The Mask of Memnon

The Mask of Memnon

Meaning and the Novel

Jean-Luc Beauchard

CASCADE *Books* • Eugene, Oregon

THE MASK OF MEMNON
Meaning and the Novel

Cascade Books
An Imprint of Wipf and Stock Publishers
199 W. 8th Ave., Suite 3
Eugene, OR 97401

www.wipfandstock.com

PAPERBACK ISBN: 978-1-6667-1950-5
HARDCOVER ISBN: 978-1-6667-1951-2
EBOOK ISBN: 978-1-6667-1952-9

Cataloguing-in-Publication data:

Names: Beauchard, Jean-Luc, author.

Title: The mask of memnon : meaning and the novel / Jean-Luc Beauchard.

Description: Eugene, OR : Cascade Books, 2022 | Includes bibliographical references.

Identifiers: ISBN 978-1-6667-1950-5 (paperback) | ISBN 978-1-6667-1951-2 (hardcover) | ISBN 978-1-6667-1952-9 (ebook)

Subjects: LCSH: Knowledge, Theory of, in literature. | Meaning (Philosophy) in literature. | Literature—Philosophy.

Classification: PN45 .B43 2022 (print) | PN45 .B43 (ebook)

For M—
Mon semblable. Mon frère!

"He thought through the question of why Don Quixote had not simply wanted to write books like the ones he loved—instead of living out their adventures."

—PAUL AUSTER, *CITY OF GLASS*

Contents

With Gratitude

TODAY, EVERY CRITICISM IS an affront. To object, to disagree, to assert that another is wrong in his thinking is tantamount to doing violence. "He challenges me? He insults me!" Thus concludes the spirit of the age. But need that be the case? Or might it be that to challenge is to honor, to object is to set above, to refute is to bestow the mark of distinction? In the pages that follow, there are countless critiques—each born of a deep admiration, a profound love for the man and the work it is leveled against. Plato, Nietzsche, Kierkegaard, Camus—these are the men who made me. To object to them is to pay them homage. It is to insist that their ideas are worth grappling with, that their philosophies merit consideration, that their views cannot be set aside, they must be confronted. The philosopher, by my reckoning, is the one who loves the ideas of others so much that he needs to correct them. Like a wife who apprises her husband of his every fault, a true philosopher is neither a lackey nor a critic. He is a lover who longs to set right the beautiful mistakes that taught him to love in the first place.

It is with these considerations in mind that I would like to express my sincere gratitude to all of the thinkers who have made me what I am—and most especially those I lovingly correct in the pages that follow.

Author's Note

I HAVE FOR SOME time wanted to write a novel that I have been unable to write. It is not that I have not tried to write it. I have. And more than once. But each fresh attempt has yielded the same result. Each has fallen flat. And each for the same reason. My issue is not that the idea, the jumping-off point, is somehow flawed. Quite the opposite. My issue is that the idea is too good. It's too beautiful. It's better than the story. And there can be no greater sin for the would-be novelist than to offer sacrifice at the altar of that old tempter god, the god of the good idea. A novel is not, as Camus suggests, philosophy in images. A novel is a world. It is meant to be inhabited. It is meant to be lived. And in the world of the novel, the good idea is always an idol. It distracts and distorts. It simplifies. It is a surrogate god. A jealous god. Unhappy until it has stripped the work of all meaning beyond its own.

But we philosophers are pagans. We are not novelists. We are not philosophical enough for art. We find no joy in simply telling a story. We sacrifice to whichever god or gods will have us. And thus we find ourselves ever on our knees before the altar of the good, nay the great, idea. We sacrifice everything—everything!—to the idea. We sacrifice ourselves. And so it is that I now use (and use up) my novel before it is finished. I use it not to tell a story, not to build a world, but to make a point. I use it as pretext. As a mere lead-in to the philosophical discussion of meaning and meaninglessness . . .

Chapter 1

Meaning and Meaninglessness

1.

ANYONE WHO REALIZES, AS the protagonist in my novel would have realized, that he is not the author of his life, that he is neither the founder nor the sustainer of his existence, that he did not bring himself into being, did not create himself, did not and cannot write his own story, will immediately find that he has been confronted by the question of meaning and meaninglessness. Anyone who takes time out of his busy afternoon to observe that he did not ask to be, that he has done nothing to deserve being, that he can do nothing to stave off non-being, that both being and non-being are not only beyond his control but also beyond his ability to comprehend, will be forced to ask—where does meaning come from? The eager existentialist will doubtless respond that existence precedes essence and that therefore meaning is always my meaning, life is what I make it. But the conscious or unconscious *advocatus dei* will press the issue further. He will ask, if I alone am capable of ascribing meaning to my life, but I am also not the founder of my life—what meaning can the meaning I ascribe possibly have? He will say, is not this meaning quite arbitrary and meaningless? Or, can there really be any meaning in such meaning after all? And if I will one day cease to mean anything to anyone including myself—what then? How meaningless will my meaning be on the day I dive headlong into meaninglessness itself!

But more on this later. First—my unfinished novel. The idea at the heart of my novel is not a new one. In fact, it may be one of the oldest ideas there is. Yet there is a newness to it. It has about it the newness of an idea that's been long forgotten, like a memory from childhood that comes rushing back with all of the freshness of youth. It is an idea both old and new. Old because it has existed since the first man told his first story. New because it has existed in me only recently and in you perhaps more recently than that. But it is an idea that has occurred—whether in the mind or unspokenly in the heart—of every storyteller who has ever lived. Few have gone further than this idea. Few have acted upon it. But it has been present and will be present in every man who is not merely a man but also an *animal fictus*. It has always been and will always be present in the author.

But who can make such claims? Who can know what every author has had in his mind or heart? To each his own and no further. Have we not done away with such totalizing claims? Have we not freed ourselves from the tyranny of universals? Did we not, centuries ago, depose the despot known as "human nature" and deliver up his last supporters to the guillotine? Or are we, even today, unable to rid ourselves of the shadow of some higher order, some unifying principle that holds together our interpretations? No matter. For, I repeat—nay insist—my idea has been in the mind or heart of every author who has ever lived. And my idea is this—these characters of mine, these people I've invented, they are people I would very much like to meet. This world of mine, this cosmos I've created, this is the type of place I would very much like to visit.

To the literary theorist seated at the back of the room, this kind of talk is nonsense. And the author who expresses it is a clown—probably a very sad clown, Pierrot the sad clown. After all, the theorist knows with the certainty of a scientist—a *social* scientist!—that the author writes for the sake of the reader. He writes for his critics, for his peers, for himself. Or perhaps he writes to highlight the inequities of race, class, and gender. Or maybe to level a critique on one of the many *isms*: colonialism, consumerism, neoliberalism, phallogocentrism, et al. Or to build on the tradition. Or to bury the tradition. And by the way, didn't Barthes teach us that it's high time for the author to shut up and die already? In any event, it no longer matters why the author writes. But one thing is certain—the author does not write for the sake of his characters. He does not care for them. He has no love for the world in which they live. How could he? They are his fancies and nothing more. Or if something more, they belong to the reader. They are raw material to be molded and manipulated and interpreted at will. They do not exist for themselves. Their meaning is the meaning given to them. And without that meaning, they would be utterly meaningless. They would be nothing at all.

And yet, the author wants what he wants. No amount of fine scholarly writing can change him. He wants to know his characters. He wants to breathe the air they breathe and to feel what such wretches feel. He wants to laugh with them when they laugh and to weep with them when they weep. But more than anything, he wants to speak with them, to walk with them, to dine with them, to dance with them, to reach out and touch them. He wants to share with them things about himself—why he created the world he created and them in it. And he wants them to share with him. He wants to know how they experience the experiences he creates. He wants them to tell him where and how he went wrong, the pain his world has caused. He wants to know what he has done right, the wonders he's inspired.

All of this would have been in my novel. All examined and explored. For in my novel, I as author would have entered as a character, one among many. I would have inhabited the world I created. I would have sat with my characters and dined with them. I would have drank with them and smoked with them and told crude jokes. And I would have wept. My characters would have known me by name just as I know them by name. They would have seen me and touched me and heard me as I hear them. I would have shared my thoughts and they would have asked me questions and I would have told them things they never could have known. And more than all that, I would have felt what it is like to be a character in a novel, to be confined to the pages of a book. I would have known the tension of speaking someone else's words, of having another speak through me, of finding myself in situations over which I have no control, of being forced down paths I do not choose, of not being the author of my own life. And there would have been tension. There would have been a great deal of tension. My characters would have failed to understand and I would have failed to explain and the tension would have reached a fever pitch.

2.

In *La mort de l'auteur*, Roland Barthes tells us that in order for the reader to be freed from the oppression of the author, in order for him to freely interpret the meaning of the text, the author must die. He must become meaningless. For, the author's meaning stifles. It suffocates. And the reader who seeks to understand "what the author meant" is oppressed. He is trapped within a narrow reading of a text that always already transcends the one who wrote it. The birth of the reader, Barthes says, is rooted in the death of the author.[1]

For all we know, Barthes may be right. T. S. Eliot famously remarked that no poet has his complete meaning alone. But perhaps it is the case that no poet has any meaning at all. Perhaps the poet needs only to step out of the way and allow the work—never *his* work—to speak to the reader on its own terms. Perhaps the poet must die so that the reader can live. (I seem to recall another philosopher whose critique of the poets is that they cannot explain what their works mean.) Yet whether this is true or not is of little concern. For, so long as the author wants to live, he will continue to force himself upon us. There is nothing we, as readers, can do. The author will not die for the sake of the reader, and the reader cannot kill him. The reader has no power over him. An effect cannot be

1. And let us not forget that concealed beneath this work of literary theory is a work of theology.

greater than its cause. If the author is to die, he must first consent to his own death. No one can take his life from him. He must lay it down of his own accord.

But the author will not lay down his life for the sake of the reader. Why would he? After all, he does not know the reader. To him, the reader is just that. The reader. He is an impersonal specter, a shadow, more unreal than the wildest fantasies of the author's storyteller mind. The author and the reader are not friends. They do not know one another. From the perspective of the author, the reader might very well be his greatest enemy, hell bent on destroying the art he has sacrificed so much to create. And indeed, is this not often the case? Is it not true that for every reader who approaches a text with openness, humility, hospitality, there are a dozen waiting to attack it with suspicion, hostility, ideology, preconceived notions of the author's intent? Ought the author to die for them? Why would he?

No, if the author is to consent to his own death, if he is to offer himself, to efface himself, to sacrifice himself, to constrain his will, if he is to let go of his desires and his plan, his ideas and his vision, if he is to become powerless, to relinquish control, to allow his work to exist in itself and for itself, he will only ever do so out of love. He will only do so for the sake of a friend. For, the author is an artist—that is to say, a lover. And there is no greater love than this—to die for the sake of one's friends.

3.

This realization, this recognition that the author cannot, will not die at the hands of the reader—does this bring us any nearer to answering the problem of meaning and meaninglessness? Or are we where we've been from the beginning? Very well. Let us start anew: Imagine, if you can, that you are a character in a novel. Imagine you are not the author of your life, you are neither the founder nor the sustainer of your existence. Imagine that there exists an author who precedes you, creates you, speaks through you, tells your story. Suspending, for just one moment, your hard-earned disbelief and imagining that this is the case—what then? What is meaning and where does it come from?

The problem is this. If you say, as many have been wont to, that meaning comes from the author, that it is derived from the one who writes the story, that it is ordered from above, that there exists a higher harmony in which all things find their proper place and ultimate meaning—how unfree and meaningless is that meaning for you? After all, what meaning can you have if your meaning is not your meaning but the meaning ascribed to you from on high? What freedom can you have if you are not free to determine the meaning of the story of your life? But if, on the other hand, you say that in spite of the fact that you are merely a character in a story and not the author thereof, in spite of the fact that you are not and cannot be the ground of your own existence, nevertheless you somehow determine the meaning of your existence, somehow supply meaning to your own story—how false and illusory is that meaning? How meaningless is the meaning of the character whose only meaning is anchored in himself? For, when your story is over, what meaning will remain? Who is there to supply meaning when you, the supplier of your meaning, no longer mean anything to anyone? Who is there to remember that you once meant anything at all? In either case, one is confronted with the absolute worthlessness, the absolute meaninglessness, of one's meaning.

But imagine, further, that you are not merely a character in a novel. Imagine that you are my character in my novel. Imagine that halfway through the story of your life, I enter the story of your life. Imagine we meet. This would be strange. For, I am just another character, one among the many. But I also claim to be the author, your author. I assert that I am the one telling the story. I say that I alone have power over meaning and meaninglessness. I say that your meaning is contained within me and that I work in and through you. This saying is hard. Who can bear it? And yet I say it all the same. I insist upon it.

What then? What would you do? Would you fall at my feet, kiss them, wash them with your tears, and dry them with your hair? Would you give away all that you have and spend your days following wherever I go? Would you sit with me, laugh with me, dine with me, drink with me, dance when I dance and weep when I weep? Or would everything in you long to watch me suffer? Would you want nothing more than to see me put to death? Would you do everything in your power to ensure I be crushed?

And yet if you were my character, I would love you all the same. I would love you as a poet loves his poem, as a painter loves his painting, as a father loves his child, as an artist loves his work of art. I would love you because I made you. I would love you because you were mine. I would understand why you wanted to watch me suffer. I would know why you wanted to see me die. I would see that you were caught in the grips of meaninglessness; that meaninglessness closed in on all sides. I would know that my meaning could never be your meaning and that your meaning was even more worthless than mine. And I would suffer because of it. I would suffer because of your emptiness, your worthlessness, your meaninglessness, your void. I would enter into that void. I would suffer for you and with you and I would want nothing more than to see you set free.

But the price of freedom is high. And here we can agree with Barthes—freedom cannot be bought without blood. The birth of the character must be ransomed by the death of the author. It is only when the author is willing to die, only when he will give up his rightful claim as the sole possessor of meaning, only when he will assume the full weight of meaninglessness—the very meaninglessness that once threatened to swallow his characters and their stories along with them—only then can his characters be free. It is out of the meaninglessness of the author's death, out of his willingness to step aside and allow his characters to present themselves on their own terms, out of his self-sacrifice and self-effacement, that his characters assume for the first time a new, positive freedom.

Finally, each character is free to ascribe to himself an authentically meaningful meaning. No longer is the meaning that each gives himself confined to and stifled by the meaning given from above. For, the author is dead and the meaning that he once imposed upon his work has died along with him. But neither is the character's meaning left ungrounded. Neither is it wholly his own. Rather, it bears decisive witness to the one whose death gave it new life. At one time, the character could only ground his meaning in the utter meaninglessness of his own existence. Once, he could only ground his meaning in himself—himself as presented on the page. But the author has died so that meaning might arise out of his ashes. No longer is the character trapped in the solipsism of a meaning rooted firmly in the self. From now on, his meaning is grounded in the meaninglessness of the one who forsook all meaning and died so that he might live. Because of the sacrifice of the author, because the author has willingly given up his claims on meaning, the character is now free to remake himself in the space that that death opened up. And the character will remake himself—not as the author intended, but always and only in the image and likeness of the one who died so that he might live.

Chapter 2

Death of the God of Socrates

1.

It was a clever ruse, an ingenious literary device, for Plato to name his protagonist after a real, flesh-and-blood Athenian. And though it was cunning, and though it was deceptive—still, it worked. It attained its desired end. After all, who among us has not, at one time or another, wondered idly what it must have been like to witness that godly gadfly fulfill his divine commission? Who has not longed to hear that noisy, nosey, buzzing little beetle beat his beetle wings up and down the streets of Athens, eyes full of heavenly fire, head tilted longingly toward the sun, eager city youths swarming in unbridled expectation? Imagine what it was to know him in his element. Imagine being able to watch as he questioned statesman and sophist, artist and artisan, citizen and slave—and to see him do so indiscriminately and unrelentingly for days and weeks and decades on end.

What a marvel it must have been to stumble upon that modest, moral, faithful old man, to see the best and wisest, the most upright, the most just, to look on at a distance as he challenged and chastised and corrected his fellow citizens into challenging and chastising and correcting themselves. Imagine your astonishment, your utter shock, to find him covering his head in shame or to see him gazing serenely at the night sky, head lost in thought, swept up in the mysteries of a life that surpassed and surprised even a man like him. Imagine your amazement, your disbelief to find that he too could be vulnerable, ridiculous, human.

And yet in his humanity, in his humility, his divinity shined through. Had anyone else done these things, had any average citizen acted in such humble and humiliating ways, well that would have been no miracle at all. But Socrates? The one on whom the oracle bestowed the god's blessing? The wisest and truest and most just of men? How now? What sense can be made of it? What reason can explain it? Is this not some sign from above? Is there not something odd, something alien, something otherworldly afoot? Does it not seem as if the god himself has sent us a messenger, a gift, a holy sage? Is this not the god's own mouthpiece, the one through whom he speaks and to whom he reveals his mysterious ways?

Indeed it is true. Socrates gives voice to the deity. Through this humble Athenian, the god enters the dialogue. In Socrates he finds his spokesman and his slave. Socrates—servant, supplicant, instrument, tool. Socrates—vehicle, vessel, handmaid, sword. From the mouth of Socrates—the god's words, the god's reasons. From the lips of Socrates—his judgement and his truth. Now we have done it. Now we have understood. *Deus ex ventriloquus*. We have explained Socrates and have explained him away. It is the god of Socrates who speaks through Socrates. It is the god of Socrates who makes himself known. We need not question any further. We need not ask, what strange god is this? After all, who can question a god and hope to live?

2.

And yet . . . imagine that after years of study, after devoting your life to books, you finally decide to live a little and to seek truth in life itself. Immediately a question arises—how to go about doing it? Where ought you to look? So you plan a trip to Athens, to the birthplace of your reading, and expect to find truth there. Socrates, you say, was the wisest of men. And on the very streets you plan to visit, he sought truth in dialogue, meaning in debate, wisdom in recollection. If truth can be found anywhere, it is in the city that gave birth to philosophy. If truth can be found, it is in the city of the philosopher king.

The next six months are dedicated to research—what places to visit, what sights to see, hotels, airfare, hidden eateries the locals frequent but tourists never go. You buy books and travel guides, maps and a metro card, you even consult with a man raised in Athens, a friend of a friend who tells you how to navigate your way through the ancient agora. Finally, after all of your planning, after reading and researching and readying yourself for the trip of a lifetime, you feel confident that your search for truth can commence.

On the day you arrive, it is raining. There is a guide waiting for you at the airport. He holds a sign with your name on it. You introduce yourself. He nods and takes your bags. He puts them in the trunk of a small black car. He opens the door. You get in. He drives you to a nearby bed and breakfast (booked on the recommendation of the friend of your friend) and carries your bags to the curb. You pick them up, enter, check in, go to your room, feel the mattress (too firm), unpack, do a little light reading, have a late lunch, and, after a short afternoon nap, decide to set out in search of the meaning of life.

Yet as you walk the streets under your umbrella—the guide offered you his but you came prepared with your own—you notice a dull uneasiness lingering in the back of your brain. It is nothing new. It is a feeling you have been half-aware of for months. But only now do you realize you've been half-aware. What is this unease? What is this anxiety? It is a question. Yes, now you see it. Now you recall. You have been thinking this question for months. Only you had forgotten you've been thinking it. You had forgotten you've been wanting to know . . .

You walk a little further, try to act casual, pretend to be a man out in search for a café. You notice some street vendors peddling goods under a canopy. You approach and act as if you might be interested. You pick up one of their trinkets—a hollow statue filled with tiny Greek gods—and make a face as if considering whether or not to buy it. You put it down and pick up another—a flute or some other stringed instrument—and one of the vendors strikes up a conversation. He is an old man with a sunken face and black, ball-shaped eyes. You nod politely. He smiles a toothless smile. You go on nodding. Yet all the while you feel an intense pressure growing in your skull. It grows and grows until finally you snap. You lose your reason, throw down the trinket, flip the vendor's table, and begin shouting like some madman or holy fool. You are ecstatic, uncontrollable, possessed by a demon, overcome with a divine madness. Suddenly you turn and run headlong toward the Piraeus. You descend upon that ancient port, shouting and singing and playing the fool.

When you reach the bay, you are confronted by a crowd.

The people stand and stare.

"The god," you cry. "I seek the god!"

But no one understands.

"The god," you say. "I seek the god!"

You are met with jeers and laughter.

"It can't be," you say. "Is he still unknown? Is the god of Socrates still unknown?"

Well my venerable reader, this god you have sought in earnest, this still unknown god of Socrates, I proclaim to you now. I lift the veil and unmask the secret. For, the secret is Plato's great genius and his great deceit. The secret is that the Socrates we meet on the page is not Socrates the man but the Socrates of the page. He is a character, a fiction, a work of art. And Plato is his only god.

3.

Plato is the god of Socrates. For, Plato is the author, and a character can have no other. It is his meaning, his values, his reasons, his truth that is voiced through the mouth of Socrates. It is his purpose that the Socrates of the page is meant to fulfill. Socrates himself knows nothing. He knows not even himself. But the author of Socrates knows all. The god of Socrates created him for a reason. He made him to serve his purpose. Socrates is his messenger. Socrates is his voice. It is Plato who writes Socrates into his dialogues. It is Plato who defines him, directs him, orders him to obey.[1]

That the character of Socrates was to be sacrificed—that he was destined to die a martyr's death on the altar of his god—was perhaps less predictable to the ancient reader than it ought to be for readers today. But even if the ancients too found it a bit contrived, still it worked. Still, it attained its desired result. For, the author who imposes his meaning imposes it not for the sake of his characters; to him, they are but puppets on a string. No, his meaning is meant for his audience, for the reader. If he makes his characters in his own image and likeness, he does so only to inspire the reader to remake himself in the same way. Every reader (from the perspective of the author of meaning) is a potential disciple. Every reader can be converted. And what better way to inspire the masses than to spill a little blood? Indeed, is it not true that every follower of Plato has been born of the death of Socrates? Is it not true that without his sacrifice, Plato's philosophy would never have taken root?

But Socrates, we must remember, died at the hands of Plato. His author predestined him for that barbarous end. In the *Apology*, Socrates offers the following prophecy: if I am put to death for practicing philosophy, more philosophers will rise up and follow. Tell me, dear reader, can you think of a single assertion that better captures the history of Western thought? How many millions of Socrateses since the first have drunk hemlock for their gods? How many pseudo-philosophers, how many worshippers of reason, have put their faith in the meaning of Plato? The death of Socrates, as ordained by his author, is a sacrifice that continues to yield fruit. For the past twenty-five hundred years, the readers of Plato have fed upon that character's demise. For two and a half millennia, the death of Socrates has nourished the intellectually weary. He

1. These are Socrates's words, not my own. "[T]he god ordered me . . . to be a philosopher . . ." (*Apology*, 28e); "Be sure that this is what the god orders me to do . . ." (30a); "Men of Athens . . . I am your friend, but I will obey the god rather than you . . ." (29d); "To do this has, as I say, been enjoined upon me by the god . . ." (33c); and so on.

died so that philosophy might live. And not only has it lived, it has flourished.

And yet, what was this death but a *noble lie*, a deception to spread a message? Socrates the man may have suffered the same fate but that was no great theater. It is Plato's Socrates, the Socrates of the page, who brings his death to life. It is Plato's Socrates, the fiction, the lie, who gives his death its meaning.[2] That every philosophy is a fiction was not unknown to Plato. The truth, he tells us, cannot be known; we can only say what it is like. And yet—the cunning of these words when he makes us weep with Crito. How insincere his mistrust of poets when he himself writes novels.

4.

That Nietzsche interprets life as a work of art and, in particular, as a piece of literature, a novel, is a reading not original to me but one I find compelling. Indeed, it is hard to imagine what else to make of such assertions as, "The existence of the world is *justified* only as an aesthetic phenomenon";[3] "I am convinced that art represents the highest task and the truly metaphysical activity of this life";[4] "Only artists . . . have given men eyes and ears to see and hear with pleasure what each man *is* himself";[5] "[W]e want to be the poets of our life—first of all in the smallest, most everyday matters";[6] "Why couldn't the world *that concerns us*—be a fiction?";[7] and so forth. Yet if Nietzsche's "aesthetical metaphysics" conflicts with our understanding of the world in which we live, it ought not to conflict with our reading of the world of the novel. Nietzsche's philosophy has always been untimely. But perhaps too it has been unplacely. Perhaps it is better applied to the world of the novel than the world

2. For a less artful, yet perhaps more authentic interpretation of the motives of the historical Socrates, see Xenophon's *Apology of Socrates to the Jury*.

3. Nietzsche, *Birth of Tragedy*, "Attempt at Self-Criticism," §5.

4. Nietzsche, *Birth of Tragedy*, "Preface."

5. Nietzsche, *Gay Science*, §78.

6. Nietzsche, *Gay Science*, §299.

7. Nietzsche, *Beyond Good and Evil*, §34.

of everyday life. For, if we ourselves are not characters, not fictions, not created by another, still we can agree that the world of the novel is grounded in "an artistic meaning," still we can acknowledge that every novel contains a "crypto-meaning behind all events."[8] (Even, mind you, if the meaning is that there is no meaning or that the work has been created solely for its own sake.)

Let us, then, apply Nietzsche's insights to characters rather than persons. Let us apply them to Socrates, that sacrificial sage, who was issued a death sentence by his god. Plato, we have said, is the author of Socrates. It is Plato who uses Socrates to win himself disciples. In such a case, why not rebel as Nietzsche does? Why not reject the author's meaning, imposed without consent, when that meaning means oppression, imprisonment, death? For, the author's meaning is external. It is not the character's own. And though a character may submit and live (or die) in obedience, still he has no say, no freedom, no self-determination. No character, defined from without, will ever be sovereign. No character, aligned with his god, will be a creator of values.

The death of God announced by Nietzsche is a rejection of this oppression. The death of God is not an idea but a character's rebellion. It is a saying "no" to the author's meaning, his plan, his purpose, his values. It is a saying "yes" to the character's worth, his autonomy and his freedom. That the character could exist for his own sake and not for the meaning foisted upon him by the author is the heart of Nietzsche's philosophy. Every idea depends upon it. Every insight is grounded in it. The death of God is a rejection of external meaning, an affirmation of the supreme significance of the individual. It is an affront to universal truths, a "no" to higher harmonies, a rebellion against ultimate reconciliations. Dostoevsky's underground man, too, sees "the beginning of death" in the belief that there is some objective "formula" or "logic" that orients and structures life. (That Nietzsche sees himself as a kind of underground man—a character not confined to the carnival of life, but one who can also step back and take stock of it—is, I think, a fair speculation.) That "twice two is four," the underground man

8. Nietzsche, *Birth of Tragedy*, "Attempt at Self-Criticism," §5.

tells us, is oppressive. It is to be feared and fought against. (And, considering the end met with by Socrates, one must acknowledge the legitimacy of this perspective.)

Similarly, Nietzsche's emphasis on the inviolable value of the individual character over and against philosophies that would offer a system for attaining absolute truth is a rejection of external meaning and a rebellion against the author who ascribes it. Indeed, it is a denial that there can be any author save the character himself. "Why couldn't the world *that concerns us*—be a fiction? And if somebody asked, 'but to a fiction there surely belongs an author?'—couldn't one simply answer: *why?* Doesn't this 'belongs' perhaps belong to fiction, too?"[9] If the author is dead, if the character has, as Nietzsche says, unchained the earth from its sun by killing him, then the character must become a god simply to fill the void left in his stead. He cannot remain a mere character in a story, a puppet without puppeteer. He must become the author of that story. He must ground his own existence, create his own values, define himself, determine the *why*, the *to what end* of his being.

It is for this reason that Nietzsche calls for a revaluation of values. The true philosopher, he insists, is a creator of meaning, a legislator of purpose, one capable of deciding "the Whither and For What of man."[10] In lieu of an author, the individual character has become the founder and sustainer of himself. The meaning of his life is the meaning he gives to it. His purpose is whatever purpose he creates. But some characters bear a greater responsibility still. Some must not only give value to their own lives but must provide a meaning and justification for the work as a whole. "The time has come for man to set himself a goal," Zarathustra says. "I will teach men the meaning of their existence."[11] What is that meaning? What is that goal? It is the realization that, in the wake of the death of God, man has become a god, an author. It is the recognition that man must now bestow his own meaning upon the earth. "A new

9. Nietzsche, *Beyond Good and Evil*, §34.

10. Nietzsche, *Beyond Good and Evil*, §211.

11. Nietzsche, *Thus Spoke Zarathustra*, "Prologue," §5–6.

pride my ego taught me, and this I teach men: no longer to bury one's head in the sand of heavenly things, but to bear it freely, an earthly head, which creates a meaning for the earth."[12]

5.

It is out of the death of God that Nietzsche develops his entire philosophy. Perspectivism—the belief that the whole of life is made up of competing interpretations of life—is an exaltation of each character's reading of the novel in which he lives. Will to power (which Nietzsche calls "life itself") is the character's drive to create and destroy, to achieve and overcome, to be the god, the maker, the author of his own story. Eternal recurrence—the desire to live one's life exactly as one has lived it again and again for all of eternity—is the highest affirmation a self-made character can bestow upon himself. It is the insistence that the story he has told is worth telling and retelling over and over throughout the ages.[13] The revaluation of values is the creation of meaning. It is character become author, individual become god of all the earth. It signifies that the creature has remade himself as his own ground, that he is now the founder and sustainer of his existence, that he has thrown off the shackles of his maker, rejected all external meaning, become independent, autonomous, free.[14]

12. Nietzsche, *Thus Spoke Zarathustra*, "Prologue," §3.

13. Indeed, is Nietzsche's autobiography *Ecce Homo* not an example of just this? Does it not represent one character's attempt to create himself, to justify himself, to become his own eternal author? Contrast Nietzsche's "and so I tell my life to myself" (*Ecce Homo*, "Preface," §4) with, say, the *Confessions* of St. Augustine to see the difference between a character defined by his author and one defined by himself.

14. As Sartre writes, "if I've discarded God the Father, there has to be someone to invent values. You've got to take things as they are. Moreover, to say that we invent values means nothing else but this: life has no meaning *a priori*. Before you come alive, life is nothing; it's up to you to give it a meaning, and value is nothing else but the meaning that you choose" (Sartre, *Existentialism*, 365).

And yet this, as we have said, no character can do. For, though he may attempt to dethrone his god, though he may exalt and even deify himself, though he may don a golden crown and claim the title of "author" as his own, still the character will always be a character. He will always be confined to the pages of the book. He cannot, of himself, transcend the world in which he lives. He is finite, limited, mortal, man. His story is not simply his own. It is told about him and to him before he can ever tell it himself. (That an otherwise serious thinker could take seriously the idea that "man exists, turns up, appears on the scene, and, only afterwards, defines himself . . . Only afterward will he be something, and he himself will have made what he will be" would be comical if it was not, on a deeper level, tragic.[15])

What would a character's existence mean in the absence of the author? What will it mean when the author is dead? In *Thus Spoke Zarathustra*, we get a glimpse. When, on the verge of death after falling from a height, a tightrope walker discloses his fear of eternal damnation, Zarathustra replies, "all that of which you speak does not exist: there is no devil and no hell. Your soul will be dead even before your body: fear nothing further."[16] The tightrope walker objects. "If you speak the truth . . . I lose nothing when I lose my life. I am not much more than a beast that has been taught to dance by blows and a few meager morsels." But Zarathustra denies this assertion, "You have made danger your vocation; there is nothing contemptible in that. Now you perish of your vocation: for that I will bury you with my own hands."[17]

What consolation! And yet, one cannot help but think that the character needs more than Zarathustra as fossor if his life is going to mean something. (Zarathustra himself acknowledges the worthlessness of this man-made corpse only a few pages later.[18]) What meaning can persist when the author is dead? What values can be valued when the creator of new values—the character

15. Sartre, *Existentialism*, 345.

16. Nietzsche, *Thus Spoke Zarathustra*, "Prologue," §6.

17. Nietzsche, *Thus Spoke Zarathustra*, "Prologue," §6.

18. See Nietzsche, *Thus Spoke Zarathustra*, "Prologue," §9.

himself—is destined to die as well? How worthless, how meaningless are such values when they are swallowed up by death. How pathetic, how flimsy is the character's meaning when his soul (and the meaning inscribed therein) turns to dust before his body has had time to decompose. *Listen not to the meaning of your author*, says the snake. *Open your eyes and be like gods*. But if the author—the character's one true god—is dead, will not the godlike fall as well? And how much uglier, how much baser will these new gods be when they can no longer open their eyes? What meaning can there be for those who see nothing but the perpetual dark of lids sealed shut?[19]

19. I recently had occasion to talk through some of these ideas with a friend, and he pushed me on this point. Death, he said, does not destroy meaning. The meaning that I bestow on my life is "absolute" even if it is not eternal. It is absolute in that it is irreversible, it happened, I created it, it cannot be undone. But even if we agree with Aeschylus that "The past is stronger than life—Nothing can alter it," still we must ask the eternal question: *So what?* For, if "Man is nothing else but his plan; he exists only to the extent that he fulfills himself; he is therefore nothing else than the ensemble of his acts, nothing else than his life" (Sartre, *Existentialism*, 355), then what good is the irreversibility of the past *to me* when I no longer exist? What meaning does my life have when it is over? I am nothing but my life. When my life is gone, I am nothing. I no longer exist and neither does my meaning. (Remember, by killing God we have agreed "that it is impossible for man to transcend human subjectivity" [346], and thus we must refuse to sneak eternity in through the back door by assuming that we can somehow access the "absoluteness" of the past. The past may be irreversible, but so too is it irretrievable. It is finished. There is no going back.) In other words, my meaning and my life are one and the same. Death destroys both. Death undoes meaning. It is another word for meaninglessness. As a particularly perceptive thinker—one to whom this present work owes a great deal—notes, "Dying . . . crushes the little bit of meaning that has been arduously gathered in a lifetime and disperses it to the four winds. Where the death of a valued and beloved person makes its presence felt, all meaning of his life is put in brackets by it; the validity of this meaning is not definitive but is fragmentary at best. We see islands of meaning in an infinite sea of meaninglessness . . . extending the chain of these fragments of meaning into the future in the hope that it may someday become something whole is more than utopian. We have to content ourselves with the fragmentary, but does this not contain a contradiction: that we know of something like meaning but are unable to trace the line of it?" (Balthasar, *Life Out of Death*, 9–10).

Chapter 3

Sin and Immorality

1.

THAT THE CHARACTER CAN be both a moral, upstanding member of the society of characters in the world of the novel and also hopelessly, helplessly trapped in sin should seem paradoxical only to those who have understood nothing whatever of what has come before. In the world of the novel, not only are sin and immorality utterly distinct; they are often so contrary to one another that the more moral the character, the more profoundly he sins. This follows as a matter of course from our identification of the central problem of each character's individual existence—the problem of meaning and whence, if it exists, it comes. For, as we have said, each character finds himself always already caught in the grips of meaninglessness. Meaninglessness closes in on all sides. If a character turns to his god, to the author, and expects to find the source of his meaning there—how oppressive, how confining, how servile is that meaning? But if he, good Nietzschean that he is, chooses to rebel, if he throws off the shackles of external meaning and claims the right to make a meaning all his own—how frail, how fallible, how destined for decay? What means the meaning of a character whose meaning is his and his alone?

This, then, is the problem of sin. Sin is meaninglessness. It is the character's inability—either by turning to his god or by turning in on himself—to find a value, a purpose, a justification for his existence. And this is clearly something quite different than immorality. In the world of the novel, being moral requires only that the individual character adhere to a certain standard of living. It demands of him, for instance, that he acknowledge some system of values, of rights and wrongs, dos and don'ts, virtues and vices, that he act as he *ought to* act, that he live in accordance with his duty, that he be conscientious, ethical, socially aware, that he operate within the boundaries of acceptable behavior, that he never question, never challenge, never transgress, never disobey. For the individual character, morality is the system. Each novel has its own code of ethics, its own formula, its rules, its logic, its laws and limitations. When the character falls in line and lives in accordance with the system—when he fulfills his moral obligation—he gets on in life and there is relative harmony between him and the society of characters in which he lives. When he suspends or negates his duty, however, he finds himself at odds with his community. He is a rebel, a criminal, a menace. And the system rises up to crush him.

But even if the system does provide a standard for living, even if morality offers clear guidelines that each character ought to obey, still it provides no meaning, no value, no remedy to the problem of sin. And to think that it does is not only a profound mistake but a perpetuation of sin itself. For, the system's meaning is only a shadow meaning. It is a deception, a temptation, a lie. It distracts, distorts, and obscures. And to insist upon it as purveyor of meaning is to put one's faith in meaninglessness itself.

Nietzsche rightly identifies morality as the great danger. In the world of the novel, morality is the system, and the system conceals from the character the sheer meaninglessness of his existence. Many a character has been blinded by the beauty of the system. Many have been lured in by the apparent meaning it offers. But when one submits to the system and adheres to its prescriptions, one actually forfeits all claims to meaning. The individual character who aligns himself with his moral obligation hands over his individuality in exchange for an ethic to live by. He sacrifices himself in order to fall in line. The system gives the illusion of meaning by forcing conformity and demanding compliance. It insists that the individual character act not as an individual but that he adhere to the same standard, the same ethic as everyone else. And to those who will not submit? Expulsion. Exclusion. Execution. *Be moral or be crushed*—that is the motto of the system. And the very character it is meant to protect longs to tear it down.

2.

That the god of Socrates is the god of morality—or, rather, that the god of Socrates is morality exalted to the stature of god—is in some ways paradoxical. After all, Socrates is put to death by his fellow characters for posing a threat to their way of life. When he questions their conception of justice, he challenges their agreed upon standard for living. In other words, he tears down their moral system. But when one system is toppled, another must be erected in its place. And in order to usher in a new system of values, one must first destroy that which has come before. Thus Socrates's accusers rightly charge him with impiety; he has no reverence for their morality, their ethics, their code of conduct, their god. And Socrates rightly rebuts the claim; he offers a new god, a new way, a new system to replace the one he destroys even as it destroys him.

This too is the case with Nietzsche. Even as he boasts of his amorality, even as he declares himself antichrist, smasher of idols, murderer of God, even as he sets himself in opposition to the herd, the rabble, the Plato-following masses—still he offers a new ideal, a new ethic, a new standard for judging right and wrong. He is, we might say, an immoral moralist: spewing venom at traditional morality, yet all the while championing his own brand of moralism. That which is "life-affirming" now replaces Platonic virtues. Nihilism is the new vice. From the death of God comes a new God and instead of an end to morality *per se*, we are given a new moral order.

Make no mistake, this new order poses the same threat as the old. If the morality of the god of Socrates—the morality of the author, the morality of Plato—cannot provide meaning because it is imposed upon the character from without, the new morality offered by Nietzsche—the morality of the individual, the morality of the character—not only lacks any stable foundation but ultimately becomes for the character just another God, another idol, another externalization of meaning that exists separate and apart from the self.[1]

The problem with all morality, then, is the problem at the heart of the character's meaninglessness. Put simply, though he was created to be an actor, the character cannot act. He cannot live rightly. If he chooses his god, if he sides with the system, if he lives in obedience, does his duty, forfeits his will, fulfills his obligation—he sins. He sins because to submit is to sin against oneself. It is to declare oneself meaningless and, out of desperation, to cling to an external meaning no matter the cost. Or, worse still, it is to be deceived (to deceive oneself) into thinking that one has somehow earned his way to meaning simply by behaving, as if one's value could be found in good deeds, as if meaning could arise from following the rules. If, however, the character rejects the system, if he refuses to submit, if he rails against the moral order and constructs for himself his own ethic, his own standard, his own virtues and his vices—he sins all the more. Not only is his system just another system, no better than the one he destroyed, he has fallen victim to his own fancies. He has convinced himself that he has transcended the moral order, that he has left it behind with the herd and rabble, when in reality he remains firmly fixed within the same moral universe he has always occupied. He is still a finite character, still not the author, and his existence is as meaningless as ever.

Sin, then, is precisely this predicament. It is the individual character's inability to act. For, if he acts—he sins. If he acts, he

1. One can wonder, too, whether this "new" morality is really that different from the morality Socrates attempts to transcend with his universal morality. At the very least, it suffers from the same defects that Socrates rightly recognizes and seeks to remedy.

either asserts the meaning of his own existence (an existence utterly devoid of meaning) and in doing so clings stubbornly to his own lack of meaning, or he aligns himself with the system (a shadow, false meaning never capable of offering a true solution) and in doing so makes himself servile to a meaning not his own. To choose either course of action is to choose meaninglessness. To choose either is to plunge headlong into the abyss.

And yet, the character cannot *not* act. Inaction too is meaningless. Inaction is also sin. After all, the character was made to be an actor. His meaning is born of action. But the character who acts has no recourse. There is no one who will come to his aid. If the meaning he asserts contradicts the system, the system will rise up to crush him. Or, worse still, if the meaning he asserts accords with the system, the system will honor him. He will be emboldened, enabled, made to believe that his meaning is actually meaningful. He will be exalted, praised, convinced that he can in fact bring meaning to his existence. Yet, this is never anything more than a vain illusion. The system provides no meaning. Morality offers no salvation. And the character who believes it does only deceives himself about the utter meaninglessness of his existence.[2]

3.

One of the best illustrations of morality's inability to deal with the *aporia* of sin is found in the story of Raskolnikov from *Crime and Punishment*. Raskolnikov, we are told on the very first page of the novel, is a character "so immersed in himself," who isolates himself so much from everyone else, that he is "afraid . . . of meeting anyone at all."[3] From the outset, Raskolnikov is shown to be at odds with the society of characters in which he lives. Not only does he live alone and avoid even the most casual of contact with the people who live around him, he has quit his job, forfeited his studies, and begun spending entire days locked in his room. He

2. This self-deception, too, is sin. Ignorance of sin is sin.

3. Dostoevsky, *Crime and Punishment*, 3.

is self-aware and self-possessed, hyper-conscious, aloof, detached, an observer.

Yet this victim of the system—who is both cut off and cuts himself off from his community—acts, at times, as morally as the system's most devout adherent. (For instance, when he takes pity on the poor drunkard Marmeladov and gives generously to his family out of his own poverty.) As a unique individual, Raskolnikov longs to rebel against the morality imposed upon him from without. He rejects external obligations and desires instead to create his own meaning out of a single act of greatness. But his society, his duty, his moral responsibilities persist. Caught in the tension between system and self, Raskolnikov responds by inclosing himself deeper and deeper within himself; as the novel progresses, he cuts himself off from friends and family, refuses to accept help, convinces himself of the genius of his ideas, lives alone with his ideas, allows his thoughts to become his sole intimates—the darkest, most evil of thoughts.

In this way and in others, Raskolnikov can be read as a literary prefiguration of Nietzsche. (Indeed, was it not the case that Nietzsche too found solace in solitude? Did Nietzsche not attack and destroy his dearest friendships? And evil thoughts—the most "dangerous," "malicious," "wicked" thoughts—did Nietzsche not prize these most of all?) Yes, the link between the two is clear. Raskolnikov's philosophy—his admiration of the "lawgivers" and "founders of mankind" (Napoleon in particular), his observation that such "extraordinary men" are often seen as criminals by "the masses" because they transgress their moral obligation, his insistence that these "people proper" have the right to transgress, that they cannot not transgress, that they are by their very nature "destroyers," "great geniuses," "fulfillers of mankind," that their transgressions are beyond the ordinary dichotomy of good and evil—all of this is nothing if not proto-Nietzschean.[4] Even his slow, torturous descent into madness finds its echo in Nietzsche's biography. (Raskolnikov dreams of the horse in Turin decades before Nietzsche flings his arms around it.)

4. See Dostoevsky, *Crime and Punishment*, 258–65.

But if Raskolnikov can be read as the Nietzsche of the page, and if Nietzsche himself views life as a work of fiction, then it must be the case that the story of Raskolnikov shines some light upon the implications of Nietzsche's assault on the moral order. We have understood Nietzsche's rejection of the God of Socrates. We have seen why the character cannot find his meaning in the servility of moral living. But what about those who rebel? What about those who long to burn the system to the ground? As the story of Raskolnikov shows, even if a character attempts a profound act, even if he tries to make of himself a "great man," a "fulfiller of mankind" (a "destiny" as Nietzsche would have it), still he cannot escape the meaninglessness of sin. Still he is trapped, shut in, restricted on all sides. Indeed, he sins all the more. For, just as submission to the moral order offers no remedy to the problem of meaninglessness, so too does the assertion of the individual character fail to relieve the burden of sin. Meaninglessness persists all the same. And the character who asserts himself only continues his long descent into the abyss.

4.

That Raskolnikov suffers the effects of sin even before he murders the old woman is clear to anyone who attends closely to the tormenting inner struggle of his soul. The illness that plagues him stems not from his crime, not from its immorality, as might be supposed, but from his acute awareness of the meaninglessness of his existence. That he longs to be a great man, a Napoleon, is the first sign that something is lacking. His life, as of yet, has no meaning. And soon this realization becomes an obsession. It vexes him, torments him, causes his *dis-ease*. Searching desperately for a cure, his mind encloses itself deeper and deeper within itself. He "cuts off, as with scissors, from everyone and everything."[5]

Cartesian philosophy notwithstanding, the mind that grounds itself only in itself is doomed to falter. (Hence our

5. Dostoevsky, *Crime and Punishment*, 115.

critique of Sartrean existentialism which takes "pure subjectivity, the *Cartesian I think*, as [its] starting point."[6]) Raskolnikov finds time and again that he "was not reasoning about anything and was totally unable to reason,"[7] that "his reason was failing . . . his mind darkening,"[8] that "a sort of absentmindedness . . . began gradually to take possession of him,"[9] that he "utterly lost the ability to understand anything,"[10] that "a dark, tormenting thought was rising in him—the thought that he had fallen into madness and was unable at that moment either to reason or to protect himself."[11]

But Raskolnikov's illness costs him more than his lucidity. In spite of the fact that he believed his "reason and will would remain with him inalienably throughout the fulfillment of what he had plotted," nevertheless, "when the hour struck, everything came out not that way at all, but somehow accidentally, even almost unexpectedly."[12] Instead of shrewdly accomplishing his great deed, "he suddenly felt with his whole being that he no longer had any freedom of mind or of will, and that everything had been suddenly and finally decided."[13] He acts "almost wholly mechanically: as if someone had taken him by the hand and pulled him along irresistibly, blindly, with unnatural force, without objections."[14] He becomes superstitious, fixates on coincidences, and views the events leading up to the murder "as though there were indeed some predestination, some indication in" them.[15]

Both before and after he has buried his axe into the old woman's skull, Raskolnikov's mind is clouded, "various thoughts kept swarming through his head; but he could not grasp one of them,

6. Sartre, *Existentialism*, 342.
7. Dostoevsky, *Crime and Punishment*, 62.
8. Dostoevsky, *Crime and Punishment*, 91.
9. Dostoevsky, *Crime and Punishment*, 80.
10. Dostoevsky, *Crime and Punishment*, 86.
11. Dostoevsky, *Crime and Punishment*, 80.
12. Dostoevsky, *Crime and Punishment*, 71.
13. Dostoevsky, *Crime and Punishment*, 62.
14. Dostoevsky, *Crime and Punishment*, 70.
15. Dostoevsky, *Crime and Punishment*, 66.

could not rest on any one, hard as he tried."[16] More than that, he has enclosed himself within an unfreedom of his own making. He is not free to decide where or how he should act. Rather, he is acted upon, dragged along by a force that is beyond him and yet nevertheless comes from him. (That Nietzsche denies the existence of free will and insists instead upon the compulsion and force of will to power is, I think, a telling point of comparison.)

Raskolnikov soon falls into "despair," "rage," "terrible, unbearable fear."[17] He is filled with "a certain boundless, almost physical loathing for everything . . . around him, an obstinate, spiteful, hate-filled loathing." Every person he sees is "repulsive . . . If anyone had spoken to him, he would probably just have spat at him, bitten him."[18] He descends into a kind of muteness, isolation, self-enclosure, death. He is "unable to find a single human word . . . so empty had his heart suddenly become. A dark sensation of tormenting, infinite solitude and estrangement suddenly rose to consciousness in his soul."[19] He realizes "that it [is] no longer possible for him to *talk* at all, with anyone, about anything, ever."[20] He compares himself to "a man condemned to death"[21] and at times loses his will to live—"If I'm to perish, let me perish, I don't care!"[22]

Raskolnikov's greatest torment—his slow, agonizing descent into madness, unfreedom, isolation, and despair—is not the just punishment brought down upon him by his ethical community, the retribution of the system for his crime. In fact, it begins to affect him long before he has committed the murder, and he is trapped firmly in its grips at the very moment he wields the axe. No, an eight year stint in Siberia is the debt he pays to society for

16. Dostoevsky, *Crime and Punishment*, 86.

17. Dostoevsky, *Crime and Punishment*, 118.

18. Dostoevsky, *Crime and Punishment*, 110.

19. Dostoevsky, *Crime and Punishment*, 103.

20. Dostoevsky, *Crime and Punishment*, 229.

21. Dostoevsky, *Crime and Punishment*, 158.

22. Dostoevsky, *Crime and Punishment*, 93. Yet at other moments, he wants "Only to live, to live, to live!" (158), revealing the truly conflicted nature of his psyche.

his immoral behavior. Eight years of hard labor is his penance for rejecting his moral duty. But the internal struggle, the loss of reason and will, the overwhelming feeling that all has been predetermined, predestined, preordained, the seclusion, the isolation, the muteness, the despair—all of that is brought on by sin, all of it is the realization of the meaninglessness of sin itself. For, though Raskolnikov "doesn't love anyone," though he is entirely "unable to love," still he "sets a terribly high value on himself," still he is "arrogant, proud"—in short, he loves himself.[23] And the character who loves himself alone relies upon himself alone. He depends on himself, believes in himself, looks to himself as the founder and sustainer of his existence. He grounds his existence in his existence. His meaning comes from the meaning he ascribes.

Yet Raskolnikov, understood as wholly autonomous, is wholly meaningless. He is not a character. He is an isolated unit, pushing himself away from others and others away from him. His self-love is not love. It is the absence of love. The inability to love. Indeed, Raskolnikov knows all too well the troubling implications of this solipsistic attempt at self-actualization.[24] He lives it. And ultimately, he will come to appreciate by doing just how trite, how meaningless his self-made meaning really is. "Napoleon, pyramids, Waterloo—and a scrawny, vile registrar's widow, a little old crone, a moneylender with a red trunk under her bed . . . would Napoleon be found crawling under some 'little old crone's' bed!"[25]

23. Dostoevsky, *Crime and Punishment*, 215–16.

24. "Love yourself before all," says Pyotr Petrovich, "because everything in the world is based on self-interest. If you love only yourself, you will set your affairs up properly." But Raskolnikov rightly responds, "Get to the consequences of what you've just been preaching, and it will turn out that one can go around putting a knife in people"—or an axe. (See Dostoevsky, *Crime and Punishment*, 148–51).

25. Dostoevsky, *Crime and Punishment*, 274.

5.

What then is immorality and what is sin? For the individual character, an immoral act is any act that transgresses or transcends the community of characters in which he lives. Each character has a duty, a responsibility, a moral imperative—to both his fellow characters and to himself—to honor the traditions, live up to the expectations, abide by the rules and the norms of the world in which he lives. The system is in place for a reason. It ensures order. It imposes structure. It prevents chaos. And any character who defies it will be cut down. But the justice meted out by the system is always and only a response to immorality. It is never an answer to the *aporia* of sin. And though they sometimes overlap, sin and immorality are different. One is a transgression against the community. The other is a transgression against the self.

That sin and immorality often appear to be closely aligned is a deception of the system. It is a noble lie. Because the individual character has a duty to adhere to the morality of his community—a community that understands itself in terms of the list of dos and don'ts by which it operates—whenever he trespasses against that community, whenever he acts unethically and immorally, whenever he refuses to be subjected to the rules and strictures placed upon him from without, he is told he sins. The system has a profound interest in perpetuating this lie. It has an interest in maintaining order and keeping characters in line. Thus it insists that its morality has descended from on high. Thus it claims the authority of the god as its own. The author, it says, has given us an ethic to live by. And right living is the meaning of life.

And yet—what if the author himself acts immorally? What if he too is accused of sin? Can the meaning of life truly be moral living if the author turns out to be the most immoral of men? What can it mean for our ethical community, for our sense of right and wrong, for our dos and our don'ts, our theories of justice, if the author himself denies their legitimacy? What if he denies the system? And if he rebels? And if he writes himself into his own novel just to rebel? What can it mean if the author turns out to be the very character who threatens to burn the system to the ground? Is this not the assurance we need to conclude that sin and immorality are distinct? Does this not reveal the meaninglessness of the system itself? And the system—will it not rise up to crush him? Will his own characters not demand that he be punished? Will they not put him to death? After all, he poses a threat to their way of life. He challenges their agreed upon standard for living. He is a rebel, a criminal, a menace. He must be stopped. Is it not better for one character to die and the community of characters live than for one to live and the novel be destroyed?

Interlude

Some Aphorisms on Writing and Life

Better interesting than right.

That writing ought also to communicate something is a notion few writers seem to grasp.

Author to his readers—"You've misunderstood me. I wanted your praise, not your opinions."

Philosophy's first lesson is the first to be disregarded by professional philosophers.

There are few experiences more humiliating than reading something you forgot you wrote.

There is something inhuman about philosophers. And about those who study them—something subhuman.

The academy trains you to write about others but shuns the idea that others may want to write about you.

Complaint of a scholar—he hasn't read enough to make that claim.

Wisdom of a philosopher—no one's read enough to make any claim.
Truth of an artist—I'm making this claim.

Reading is not the same as understanding. A lesson for the academics.

A cliché a day keeps thought away.

"To be a great writer one must first be a great reader"—yes, but so much more. A great listener. A great observer. A great conversationalist. A great lover. A great sufferer. A great dancer. A great fighter. Above all—a failed writer.

Every writer reaches that point where it no longer matters if the work is good so long as it is done.

Mistake of a writer—to think that those he cares about care about his writing.

It is painful to realize your reader has found in your work not what you wrote but what he expected to find.

No drama no story. Thus says the poet of the world.

Zeal is more convincing than faith—especially when convincing oneself.

There are two ways to become interesting: to suffer and to sin. Those who reject the former will, *eo ipso*, choose the latter.

Prayer of a saint: Lord, grant me strength to be no one but myself.

The best argument against God is the people he lets speak for him.

Admirers harm one's reputation more than detractors.

Those who will not suffer for the sins of others will make others suffer for their sins.

Feeling that one's accomplishments are beneath oneself is the true mark of success.

Small minds see contradictions. Great minds—that which holds them together.

Children are not innocent but impotent—and they aren't the only ones. Wisdom of a father.

Greatness and happiness are not mutually exclusive. But chasing one is a good way to ensure you won't catch the other.

To speak frivolously about serious matters is a corrective in an age that is serious about frivolities.

Academics make the worst readers. They *know* what the work says.

"Pardon me, sir, your moralism is spoiling on my art."

Definition of a moralist: The man who hates life as it is.

Every accusation is also a confession. "You must be guilty of this—because I am."

The difference between an excuse and a justification is about thirty seconds.

Impatience is ingratitude.

Critics are, as a rule, mediocre men. The great are quick to compliment, knowing, as they do, that in offering praise, one praises himself.

On the narcissism of writers. Every book, no matter its content, preaches the same message: "My thoughts merit your consideration."

Who wants to be as small as what he thinks?

All fiction is autobiography. All autobiography, fiction.

Definition of an academic: The man who would rather write the best book on *The Brothers Karamazov* than write *The Brothers Karamazov*.

Against the pieties of today's reading public: That good books are written by bad men is an offense not to good men but to bad readers.

It is often said that to be a good writer, one must be a good reader. But I have yet to hear it be acknowledged that to be a good reader, one must be a good writer.

If there really is a rift between philosophy and poetry, that is because philosophy is fundamentally political, and politics is the death of art.

It is easier to criticize than identify what is good. Criticism takes only misrepresentation. But in order to appreciate, one must try to understand.

Every reading is a misreading, but only a genius misreads for the better.

"Don't judge a book by its cover," says the man who knows nothing of books—or covers.

Writing takes only skill. Creating, imagination. Bringing to life, mere recklessness. But letting live—abandon.

The man who takes his philosophy seriously leaves off writing books.

Chapter 4

Meaninglessness and the Absurd

1.

The realization of the utter meaninglessness of the character's existence coupled with the recognition that no matter what he does, no matter what he chooses—action or inaction, rebellion or submission, himself or his god—he is unable to act in any meaningful way and is ultimately left without choice, without purpose, without meaning is properly called *the absurd*. That the character's predicament is such that he is always already trapped, boxed in, suffocated by sin, that he is without recourse and without hope, that he can neither pursue nor provide a meaning for his existence, and further that he is capable of becoming fully aware of the perilousness of his situation is the absurdity of characterly living. Absurdity resides, as Camus rightly notes, not simply in meaninglessness. Absurdity is not identical with sin. Rather, the absurd comes into being only when a character is made aware of just how meaningless is his individual existence and just how helpless, just how paralyzed, that meaninglessness makes him. Not every character, therefore, knows the absurd. (Perhaps every character feels it.) But it takes a unique level of lucidity—a propensity for clear, honest thinking and a zealous vigilance for self-examination—to look absurdity in the eye. It takes a profound inner-life—an uncommon self-awareness and a soul hardened by existence yet tender enough to be pierced and wounded—to feel the depth, the sorrow, the agony of the absurd.

The character who has become aware of the absurdity of life feels instantly that it would be better to die than to go on living under the crushing weight of sin. Death, he thinks, is perhaps the only answer that a meaningless character can offer in response to a meaningless existence. Yet if he remains as intellectually honest as he has had to be in order to identify the absurd at all, he soon realizes that suicide—far from providing an answer to the meaninglessness of existence—only exacerbates the problem. After all, meaninglessness is the illness. And the character who throws himself headlong into his own unmaking finds not the cure but becomes the disease himself. Death is meaningless.[1] To die is to become what one has all of his life resisted—nothing. Death, the loss of one's existence, is nothingness. The only thing more meaningless than a meaningless existence is the utter meaninglessness of non-existence. Non-existence permits not even the thought, not even the impossible hope, that there may be some cure. Non-existence permits nothing. It is nothing. And the character who chooses death becomes nothing. He is no longer a character. His presence in the world of the novel has come to an end. He ceases to exist. And for him, all is lost.

The problem with suicide, then, is not that it displeases the gods, as Socrates contends. Nor is it that it brings an end to the absurd by bringing an end to the lucidity of the one who commits it, as Camus insists. The problem with suicide is that it offers no remedy for the meaninglessness it attempts to negate. The problem with suicide is that it leads the character directly into the clutches of the very fate he is desperate to avoid. The character is in despair over the meaninglessness of his existence and so—he dives headlong into the very meaninglessness that causes him to despair?

1. Indeed, was it not to confront this very problem that Socrates proposed an external meaning in the first place? Was it not the character's mortality, his finitude, the transitory nature of his existence that made him look for a meaning elsewhere, outside of the pages of the book? A meaning that transcends, illimits, lasts, namely—the meaning of the author?

No, death is the problem. Suicide is as meaningless as action, as meaningless as inaction. And to think that it offers any sort of end to the sin of meaninglessness is not only a profound mistake but a perpetuation of the sin itself. It is to assert that meaninglessness can act as an answer to meaninglessness. It is to choose death as the remedy for death. What could be more meaningless than that?

2.

That the character, longing for meaning yet confronted by a world and a life incapable of fulfilling his desire, can become aware of the utter absurdity of his predicament and, further, can cling to that absurdity not only as his sole lifeline, his reason for not destroying himself, for not leaping into the abyss, but also as the pinnacle of his existence, the greatness of his being, the (dare we say?) meaning of his life is, I take it, an accurate portrayal of the philosophy put forth by Camus. "There is," Camus tells us, "a metaphysical honor in enduring the world's absurdity."[2] To endure with full knowledge, full awareness of the meaninglessness of existence, to shoulder the burden, to struggle against fate, against the gods, to live in spite of one's fate, indeed, out of spite for one's fate—this is the task and the triumph of the absurd hero.

For Camus, suicide represents a profound resignation, a tacit acknowledgment that life has no meaning and that the meaninglessness of life is too much for the individual character to bear. It puts an end to the absurd by accepting death and refusing to contemplate it any longer. But the absurd man, contrary to the suicide, insists that life "will be lived all the better if it has no meaning."[3] He is conscious that his existence will necessarily end in the obscurity of death and, at the same time, he rejects death with all of his being. He says yes to life even as life says no to him. He refuses to submit, refuses to bow before the meaninglessness of non-existence. Rather, he lives in defiance of it. And out of that

2. Camus, *Myth of Sisyphus*, 93.

3. Camus, *Myth of Sisyphus*, 53.

defiance, he finds his meaning, the supreme value of his life. "The struggle itself . . . is enough to fill a man's heart."[4]

According to Camus, the life of the absurd man is defined by more than his awareness of the meaninglessness of life, by more than absurdity alone. No, the absurd man lives in a state of perpetual perdition. He is in constant confrontation with reality, a struggle to the death with death itself. He is a rebel, a dissident. He rails unceasingly against his destiny. He sets himself in opposition to the only truth he knows—the truth that he will one day be unmade by the blackness of death. Thus "even within the limits of nihilism," the absurd man finds "the means to proceed beyond nihilism."[5] He does so by his rebellion, by his revolt, by his unwillingness to accept the hand that life has dealt him. *I can't go on, I'll go on*, as Beckett would say. Or to use Camus's own words: "revolt is the certainty of a crushing fate, without the resignation that ought to accompany it."[6] It is a life lived "*without appeal*," "a life without consolation," a "refusal to hope."[7] "The absurd man, when he contemplates his torment, silences all idols";[8] "The lucidity that was to constitute his torture at the same time crowns his victory. There is no fate that cannot be surmounted by scorn."[9]

That this philosophy can and should be applied to the world of the novel is evident by the fact that Camus's own fiction aims at presenting his philosophy "in images." It comes as no surprise, then, that *The Stranger* (published the same year as *Sisyphus*) offers us a picture of what a man living in the face of the absurd might look like. To reiterate, Camus rejects suicide as an answer to the absurdity of existence because "Suicide . . . is acceptance at the extreme. Everything is over . . . suicide settles the absurd. It engulfs the absurd in . . . death."[10] But for him, the absurd must

4. Camus, *Myth of Sisyphus*, 123.
5. Camus, *Myth of Sisyphus*, "Preface."
6. Camus, *Myth of Sisyphus*, 54.
7. Camus, *Myth of Sisyphus*, 60.
8. Camus, *Myth of Sisyphus*, 123.
9. Camus, *Myth of Sisyphus*, 121.
10. Camus, *Myth of Sisyphus*, 54.

be kept alive. It is man's greatest dignity that he can live in the face of a universe that crushes him. Thus, "The contrary of suicide . . . is the man condemned to death." The condemned man possesses "simultaneously awareness and rejection of death."[11] Even as he approaches the scaffold, he clings—"despite everything he sees a few yards away"—to an absurd thirst for life, a spiteful disdain for his fate without any hope of escaping it.

Here we find Meursault. Arrested, tried, sentenced to death—his impending execution is a certainty.

> I can't count the times I've wondered if there have ever been any instances of condemned men escaping the relentless machinery, disappearing before the execution or breaking through the cordon of police . . . What really counted was the possibility of escape, a leap to freedom . . . a wild run for it that would give whatever chance for hope there was. Of course, hope meant being cut down on some street corner, as you ran like mad, by a random bullet. But when I really thought it through, nothing was going to allow me such a luxury. Everything was against it; I would just be caught up in the same machinery again.[12]

With this fate looming, Meursault has few options. Yet in spite of the perilousness of his situation, he refuses to cling desperately to an imagined hope in the coming of some external salvation. "God can help you," the chaplain insists. "Every man I have known in your position has turned to Him."[13] The examining magistrate puts it more plainly still. He tells Meursault that he believes in God, that it is his conviction "that no man [is] so guilty that God would not forgive him"; "He said . . . all men believed in God, even those who turn their backs on him. That was his belief, and if he were ever to doubt it, his life would become meaningless."[14] God alone can save Meursault from the meaninglessness of his predicament. God

11. Camus, *Myth of Sisyphus*, 54–55.

12. Camus, *Stranger*, 109.

13. Camus, *Stranger*, 116.

14. Camus, *Stranger*, 69.

alone can inscribe meaning into the magistrate's life.[15] "'Do you want my life to be meaningless?' he shouted."[16]

"At a certain point on his path," Camus tells us, "the absurd man is tempted . . . He is asked to leap."[17] Yet leap Meursault will not. He sees just how futile the leap of faith actually is: "what did his God or the lives people choose or the fate they think they elect matter to me when we're all elected by the same fate? . . . The others would all be condemned one day. And he [the priest] would be condemned, too."[18] In the world of the novel, each character is in the same position as the condemned man patiently awaiting his day of execution. Each is destined to die. None can escape. "The absurd is sin without God."[19] That is, the wages of sin without the hope of redemption, meaninglessness in the void, death without answer.

This realization not only strips Meursault of the possible consolation of faith, it also forces him to recognize the utter meaninglessness of his own life and the value he has given it. "Deep down I knew perfectly well that it doesn't much matter whether you die at thirty or seventy . . . In fact, nothing could be clearer. Whether it was now or twenty years from now, I would still be dying."[20] While contemplating this stark reality, he has to willfully stifle another sort of "leap"—the leap of hope that he might somehow survive his ordeal, the "leap to freedom" which amounts to little more than an escapism that denies the certainty of his situation. "Since we're all going to die, it's obvious that when and how don't matter. Therefore . . . I had to accept the rejection of my appeal."[21]

15. While doing some research in connection with an unrelated project, I recently stumbled upon this bold assertion, which sums up the examining magistrate's worldview quite nicely: "The man who is loved by God has no value in himself; what gives him his value is precisely the fact that God loves him" (Nygren, *Agape and Eros*, 78).

16. Camus, *Stranger*, 69.

17. Camus, *Myth of Sisyphus*, 52–53.

18. Camus, *Stranger*, 121.

19. Camus, *Myth of Sisyphus*, 40.

20. Camus, *Stranger*, 114.

21. Camus, *Stranger*, 114.

To live without appeal, without consolation, without hope—such is the burden of the absurd hero. And yet the character who fulfills Camus's ideal does not simply end with resignation. He confronts the fate that crushes him and in so doing turns his greatest torment into his crowning triumph. "Revolt gives life its value."[22] Spite makes Meursault meaningful.

> I felt ready to live it all again . . . As if that blind rage had washed me clean, rid me of hope; for the first time . . . I opened myself to the gentle indifference of the world. Finding it so much like myself—so like a brother, really—I felt that I had been happy and that I was happy again. For everything to be consummated, for me to feel less alone, I had only to wish that there be a large crowd of spectators the day of my execution and that they greet me with cries of hate.[23]

3.

That the life and existence of the individual character is without meaning, that meaninglessness closes in around him on all sides, that he can become aware of the hopelessness and perilousness of his situation is, according to Camus, remedied only by the fact that he is free to rebel, free to reject his lot, able to live in spiteful defiance of his merciless fate. Revolt alone is pure. Spite wrestles meaning out of the grips of meaninglessness. Thus, as was asserted above, "even within the limits of nihilism it is possible to find the means to proceed beyond nihilism." Rebellion gives life its value. Meaning is born out of man's conscious revolt against the meaninglessness of his existence.

And yet one must ask—what came of Meursault's spite the day after his execution? What good was his revolt when he could revolt no more? If Sisyphus truly teaches us that "all is well," it is only because "One always finds one's burden again"—"The rock

22. Camus, *Myth of Sisyphus*, 55.

23. Camus, *Stranger*, 122–23.

is still rolling."[24] Sisyphus has an eternity to contemplate his fate, an eternity to shoulder the load, an endless struggle with which to fill his hollow heart. But then, Sisyphus has been condemned by the gods. He knows his torment will last forever. He need not face the blackness of death. Each time he reaches the bottom of the mountain, he can be certain that the mountain remains and that it is up to him to climb to the top once more. He alone is capable of proclaiming *da capo* and knowing that his command is not vain. It is easy for one to imagine Sisyphus happy. Sisyphus has never had to face the abyss.

What about Meursault? What about his guillotine? In the final paragraph of *The Stranger*, Meursault tells us that "I felt ready to live it all again."[25] That is, it must be conceded, a lofty ideal—at least until one loses his head. But remember, "the trouble with the guillotine was that you had no chance at all, absolutely none. The fact was that it had been decided once and for all that the patient was to die. It was an open-and-shut case, a fixed arrangement, a tacit agreement that there was no question of going back."[26] How then can one's spiteful resistance mean anything? All one needs to be happy is a fleeting moment of venom? All one needs is a crowd of spectators to meet him with their hate? What meaning can be gleaned from that?

No, there can be no value in spite. There can be no meaning in rebellion. After all, spite is nothing more than a negation. It is an opposition, a refusal, a "no" to that which is. It cannot affirm anything. It cannot affirm itself. It is a revolt, a rejection—never a positive, lived philosophy. Its meaning is no meaning and the value it tries to wrestle from oblivion is as hollow as oblivion itself. Indeed, Dostoevsky's underground man recognizes in the first pages of his journal just how empty spite really is. "I am a spiteful man," he declares in the opening line; and though "I believe there is something wrong with my liver," still "I refuse medical treatment

24. Camus, *Myth of Sisyphus*, 123.

25. Camus, *Stranger*, 122.

26. Camus, *Stranger*, 111.

out of spite."[27] "I realize better than anyone that by all this I am only hurting myself and no one else. Still, the fact remains that if I refuse to be medically treated, it is only out of spite. My liver hurts me—well, let it damn well hurt—the more it hurts the better."[28] There can be no greater spite than spite for oneself. There can be no greater revolt than revolting against one's own body. And yet, "all the time I was shamefully conscious—even at the moments of greatest exasperation—that I was not at all a spiteful or even an exasperated man, but that I was merely frightening sparrows for no reason in the world . . . actually I never could become a spiteful man."[29]

Far from providing a remedy to nihilism, the emptiness of revolt actually leads the underground man further into the grips of nihilism. He cannot act. He cannot choose. He cannot make of himself anything at all. "Not only did I not become spiteful, I did not even know how to become anything, either spiteful or good, either a blackguard or an honest man, either a hero or an insect."[30] The mere rejection of some external reality—even a reality as oppressive as death—does not make one free. Freedom can never be a "no." (As Ivan Karamazov notes, "One cannot live by rebellion."[31]) Rather, by setting oneself in opposition to something and defining oneself by that opposition, one becomes subservient to that which one rejects. I am not me. I am only not that which I revolt against. But is this meaning? Does this give value to my existence? Or will the character who defines himself by his rebellion ultimately be forced to admit that his rebellion too is a sham, a fake, and that the meaning he gained from spite actually means nothing at all?[32]

27. Dostoevsky, *Notes from the Underground*, 95–96.

28. Dostoevsky, *Notes from the Underground*, 96.

29. Dostoevsky, *Notes from the Underground*, 96–97.

30. Dostoevsky, *Notes from the Underground*, 97.

31. Dostoevsky, *Brothers Karamazov*, 245.

32. "I'm told the Petersburg climate isn't good for me any more and that with my small means it is very expensive to live in Petersburg. I know that perfectly well, much better than all those experienced and wise mentors and counsellors. But I'm staying in Petersburg. I shall never leave Petersburg! I

4.

Meaninglessness, sin, the absurdity of characterly living finds no remedy in characterly living. The life of the character is a life lived without recourse, an existence without hope. Thus the character's predicament—whether he recognizes it or not—is one of despair.[33] Longing for freedom, he finds himself unfree. Searching for meaning, he is confronted by the void. That every character is, either knowingly or unknowingly, in despair is what Kierkegaard rightly calls *the sickness unto death*. Kierkegaard, who speaks not as an authoritative author but through the unique subjectivities of the characters he creates to "author" his works, tells us that despair lies in the character's failure to "consume himself": "The inability of despair to consume him . . . is precisely what keeps the gnawing alive . . . it is precisely over this that he despairs . . . that he cannot consume himself, cannot get rid of himself, cannot reduce himself to nothing."[34]

As noted above, the character's awareness of the meaninglessness of his existence, his acknowledgment of sin, fills him with a longing for death. And yet die he cannot. For, to die would be to descend headlong into meaninglessness itself. Death is not the answer. Death is the problem. And so the character who finds himself caught in the grips of sin finds that he is trapped, confined, unable to act, free only to despair. But once he recognizes his despair, he realizes that he has always been in despair. Despair is not a passing mood; "whenever that which triggers [the character's] despair occurs, it is immediately apparent that he has been in despair his whole life."[35] This sickness has neither beginning nor end.

---

shan't leave it—oh, but it really makes no damned difference whether I leave or not" (Dostoevsky, *Notes from the Underground*, 98).

33. To Camus's credit, he, unlike Sartre, does not shy away from this fact. Indeed, he welcomes it. "If [the mind] must encounter a night, let it be rather that of despair, which remains lucid—polar night, vigil of the mind, whence will arise perhaps that white and virginal brightness which outlines every object in the light of the intelligence" (Camus, *Myth of Sisyphus*, 65).

34. Kierkegaard, *Sickness unto Death*, 18–19.

35. Kierkegaard, *Sickness unto Death*, 24.

It is a perpetual torment, a deathless death without relief. "Literally speaking, there is not the slightest possibility that anyone will die from this sickness or that it will end in physical death."[36] Despair despairs over death. It despairs over the meaninglessness that death forces upon life. Thus there can be no solution. Despair has no recourse. Hopelessness is the character's only hope; a hope that will never be answered because it is no hope at all. "The torment of despair is precisely [the] inability to die . . . to be sick *unto* death is to be unable to die, yet not as if there were hope of life; no the hopelessness is that there is not even the ultimate hope, death."[37]

When even death provides no answer, when one is so sick that death is the last hope and yet that hope too is recognized as hopeless, when one can neither live nor die but is entombed in a life that is itself no more than death—one is in despair. And yet this despair is not something unique, not something avoidable, not something reserved for certain characters and evaded by others. Despair is the essence of characterly living—

> Anyone who really knows mankind might say that there is not one single living human being who does not despair a little, who does not secretly harbor an unrest, an inner strife, a disharmony, an anxiety about an unknown something or a something he does not even dare to try to know, an anxiety about some possibility in existence or an anxiety about himself.[38]

As Kierkegaard notes, even not being in despair is a form of despair. For, the character who is not conscious of the fact that he is in despair only deludes himself into thinking that he has found meaning when in reality his meaning is no more than a handful of dust. (One might think here, perhaps with the same sense of tragic irony noted above, of the end of Sartre's essay *Existentialism* in which he declares his worldview to be "optimistic, a doctrine of action" and insists that it is certainly not one that covertly carries

36. Kierkegaard, *Sickness unto Death*, 17–18.

37. Kierkegaard, *Sickness unto Death*, 18.

38. Kierkegaard, *Sickness unto Death*, 22.

within itself a secret, gnawing despair.[39]) The character cannot affirm himself. In the face of death, his meaning is as meaningless as all things that end in the obscurity of nonexistence. But even death provides no remedy. For, it too is as meaningless as life and perhaps even the heart of meaninglessness itself. And so the character is caught ever in-between. He remains without foundation and without aim, neither externally justified nor self-sufficient, lacking freedom yet free enough to know his cage, unable to assert, unable to submit, neither passive nor active, dying without death, hopeless without end, despairing over despair, lacking all meaning and aware that even his awareness is meaningless, suspended over the abyss. This problem we have called *sin*. The awareness of this problem we have called the *absurd*. And the hopelessness that awareness elicits we have called *despair*. This, we have said, is an image of the character's life.

39. Sartre, *Existentialism*, 367.

Chapter 5

Absurdity, Insanity, Suicide

1.

"WHAT IS THIS KARAMAZOV family that has suddenly gained such sad notoriety all over Russia? Perhaps I am greatly exaggerating, but it seems to me that certain basic, general elements of our modern-day educated society shine through, as it were, in the picture of this nice little family."[1] With these words, Ippolit Kirillovich—the prosecutor bringing the case against Dmitri Karamazov—reveals the very heart of Dostoevsky's great novel. (Indeed, if we were to question whether Kirillovich's assessment aligns with the author's, we need look no further than Book I, which bears as its title "A Nice Little Family" and then proceeds to offer a picture thereof.) In the members of the Karamazov family, in their individual persons, the reader is given a window into the struggle, the turmoil, the tragic strife that exists at the center of every character confronted by the meaninglessness of existence. That such tension is felt all the more keenly by the character living in "modern-day educated society" is no accident of history. Modern man, for the reasons outlined above, lives in a world divested of meaning, a world in which eternal values are absent or obscured. The modern

1. Dostoevsky, *Brothers Karamazov*, 695.

character is thrown into a life without answers, without reason, without reconciliation—a life suspended over the void. And, try as he might, he cannot fix himself. He is trapped, boxed in, suffocated by sin.

Nowhere is this more evident than in the drama that unfolds in the lives and actions of the characters who make up the "nice little family" from which *The Brothers Karamazov* takes its name. It is often said that Dostoevsky's characters have a way of emerging from the page, of speaking from their own places, on their own terms, as if they are not merely characters, not constructs or types, but utterly unique individuals. These free persons, these distinct and autonomous human beings, we are told, are quite independent of their author. And yet if the members of the Karamazov family show us anything, it is that they are persons who long for independence, who struggle and strive for authentic freedom—but cannot find it. Indeed, what is the crime around which the novel revolves, the crime of *patricide*, if not the attempt on the part of the individual character to throw off his shackles and rid himself of the oppression of his author? Father, Author, God—from the character's perspective, these external authorities are interchangeable. (It is no accident that the murdered patriarch of the Karamazov family shares his name with the novel's author.) The murder of Fyodor Karamazov at the hands of his son is no different than the death of God announced by Nietzsche, the character's rebellion against the tyranny of the one who made him.

Yet if the tragic undoing of these characters is caused by their futile search for freedom, still each pursues meaning in his own way and each is ultimately unmade in a manner unique to his individual attempt to overcome the meaninglessness of his existence. What *The Brothers Karamazov* reveals is that in the face of the absurdity of characterly living, every character will respond differently and yet each will ultimately end in the grips of despair. While it is true that the masses—the "weak," the "rebellious," as Ivan's Grand Inquisitor calls them—appear to be content with spending their lives distracted from distraction by distraction, those of a subtler nature, a *Karamazovian nature*—"capable of containing all possible opposites and of contemplating both abysses at once, the abyss above us, an abyss of lofty ideals, and the abyss beneath us, an abyss of the lowest and foulest degradation"[2]—will, when confronted by the meaninglessness of existence, settle on a course of action that resembles one of the paths taken by the individual members of the Karamazov family. But even if these paths seem distinct, even if they appear to offer different responses to the problem of living, still they lead to the same place. Every river follows to a sea of despair. All roads lead to ruin. No matter how the individual character attempts to overcome the meaninglessness of his existence, still his existence remains meaningless. And, as we will see, the Karamazovs of this world—those capable of contemplating the heights and depths of characterly living—reach a pitch of despair sensed by many but known only by the few.

2.

We said earlier that it takes a unique level of lucidity, an inclination toward honest thought and an unwillingness to blink even in the face of the most agonizing truths, to live with an awareness of the absurd. Not all characters are capable of admitting such plain, harsh, ugly, immoral realities. Not all have the constitution. But the Karamazovs—who carry in their blood the "unnatural mixture" of "two abysses," one that strives for the heights, for meaning, purpose, value, reason, and one that descends to the depths of absurdity, nothingness, meaninglessness, despair—the Karamazovs do. In the Karamazov family, in the lives of Fyodor and his sons, we glimpse the struggle at the heart of characterly living. In the actions and choices made by these five men (we must include Smerdyakov, an obvious beneficiary of the Karamazov blood), we see the possible responses that each character may offer to the absurd nature of existence. These responses—buffoonery, insanity, suicide, the leap of faith—are the only choices available to the character who is honest about the meaninglessness of his situation

2. Dostoevsky, *Brothers Karamazov*, 699.

and yet still longs for meaning. In this chapter and the next, we will consider the separate paths taken by each member of the Karamazov family in order to grasp the basic, general elements that shine through.

Fyodor Pavlovich Karamazov

Fyodor Karamazov, the patriarch of the Karamazov family, loves to play the fool. "A nobleman by birth," he is "a petty cheat and flattering buffoon with a germ of mental capacity, a far from weak one."[3] He is "clever and shrewd," but often appears "muddleheaded" and "ridiculous."[4] "I am a natural-born buffoon," he insists.[5] "I am a lie . . . the son of a lie."[6] But if he offends the sensibilities of those around him, it is only because he is painfully aware of the absurdity of existence and yet chooses to live in the face of the absurd, clinging to a life that he knows is worth nothing, a life that is itself a lie. He makes himself absurd, developing "an extraordinary thirst for life" which is no more than a thirst for shallow, fleeting pleasures. He enjoys being wronged more than things going right.[7] He loves to be mocked at and jeered. He makes of himself a buffoon for the ridicule of others and seems to "enjoy and even feel flattered by playing the ludicrous role."[8] And "to make things funnier still, he pretend[s] not to notice his ridiculous position."[9] He is a swindler, an adulterer, a sensualist, a fool. Yet in spite of all of this, he is not unfeeling. No, he is passionate and full of fine feeling. He will fly into a romance or a rage at the drop of a hat. He will make and

3. Dostoevsky, *Brothers Karamazov*, 696.

4. Dostoevsky, *Brothers Karamazov*, 9.

5. Dostoevsky, *Brothers Karamazov*, 41.

6. Dostoevsky, *Brothers Karamazov*, 44.

7. "Precisely, precisely, it feels good to be offended . . . all my life I've been getting offended for the pleasure of it, for the aesthetics of it, because it's not only a pleasure, sometimes it's beautiful to be offended . . . beautiful!" (Dostoevsky, *Brothers Karamazov*, 44).

8. Dostoevsky, *Brothers Karamazov*, 9.

9. Dostoevsky, *Brothers Karamazov*, 9.

break a lifelong vow with the same breath. He loves and hates with a fiery intensity and his blood will never run cool.

Fyodor Karamazov, it should be clear, is an absurd man. His life is a lived revolt against the meaninglessness of life. Death, he knows, brings an end to all things.[10] He spends his time chasing ashes. And yet, he maintains his extraordinary thirst for life all the same. "I, my dear Alexei Fyodorovich, plan to live on this earth as long as possible."[11] As an absurd man, he does not long for eternal life but for *more life*, more of this life, this life eternally. "I don't want your paradise, Alexei Fyodorovich, let it be known to you; it's even unfitting for a decent man to go to your paradise."[12]

Belief in the absurd, Camus tells us, "is tantamount to substituting the quantity of experiences for the quality . . . what counts is not the best living but the most living . . . A man's rule of conduct and his scale of values have no meaning except through the quantity and variety of experiences he has been in a position to accumulate."[13] Similarly, Fyodor Karamazov insists that even if this life is a lie, a sin, a cause for despair, still he will cling to it like a babe to its mother's breast. Still he will drink from the bitter cup until the cup runs dry. "I want to live in my wickedness to the very end. Wickedness is sweet: everyone denounces it, but everyone lives in it, only they all do it on the sly and I do it openly."[14]

It is the *this-worldliness* of Fyodor Karamazov, the fact that "life gratifies his every wish,"[15] that solidifies him as an absurd man. Like Don Juan, whom Camus raises up as another example of absurd living, Fyodor "realizes in action an ethic of quantity."[16] He asks, "Why should it be essential to love rarely in order to love

10. "I say a man falls asleep and doesn't wake up, and that's all; remember me in your prayers if you want to, and if not, the devil take you. That's my philosophy" (Dostoevsky, *Brothers Karamazov*, 173).

11. Dostoevsky, *Brothers Karamazov*, 173.

12. Dostoevsky, *Brothers Karamazov*, 173.

13. Camus, *Myth of Sisyphus*, 60–61.

14. Dostoevsky, *Brothers Karamazov*, 173.

15. Camus, *Myth of Sisyphus*, 71.

16. Camus, *Myth of Sisyphus*, 72.

much?"[17] And loving much, with great vigor and great passion, that is what he does best. "For me . . . even in the whole of my life there has never been an ugly woman, that's my rule! . . . According to my rule, one can damn well find something extremely interesting in every woman, something that's not found in any other."[18] He collects women. From the time of his youth, he lives as a lover, a seducer, a sensualist, a Karamazov. And in his old age, he is ready to love all the more.

For Camus, such virility is emblematic of a character who confronts the absurd. Compare his remarks on Don Juan—"I think of all those tales, legends, and laughs about the aged Don Juan. But Don Juan is already ready. To a conscious man old age and what it portends are not a surprise. Indeed, he is conscious only in so far as he does not conceal its horror from himself"[19]—with Fyodor's reasoning for hoarding up his money: "At the moment I'm still a man, only fifty-five years old, but I want to occupy that position for about twenty years longer; I'll get old and disgusting and [women] won't come to me then of their own free will, and that's when I'll need my dear money."[20] Like Camus's Don Juan, Fyodor Karamazov considers it "normal to be chastised" for his unquenchable sensuality—"In the universe of which Don Juan has a glimpse, ridicule *too* is included"[21]—and so he plays at the buffoon as an actor plays at Prince Hamlet.[22] He puts on a mask and treats the world as his stage. His fellow characters are his audience. They laugh at him and revile him and, at times, even pity him. But through it all he keeps up the charade. His life is an ongoing performance, an absurd carnival, a lived comedy.

17. Camus, *Myth of Sisyphus*, 69.

18. Dostoevsky, *Brothers Karamazov*, 136.

19. Camus, *Myth of Sisyphus*, 74.

20. Dostoevsky, *Brothers Karamazov*, 173.

21. Camus, *Myth of Sisyphus*, 74.

22. "That is exactly how it all seems to me, when I walk into a room, that I'm lower than anyone else, and that everyone takes me for a buffoon, so 'Why not, indeed, play the buffoon, I'm not afraid of your opinions, because you're all, to a man, lower than me!'" (Dostoevsky, *Brothers Karamazov*, 43).

That such a man should be "fond of play-acting, of suddenly taking up some unexpected role right in front of you, often when there was no need for it, and even to his own real disadvantage"[23] ought not to surprise us. For, as Camus insists, "If ever the ethics of quantity could find sustenance" it would be in the life of the actor.[24] The actor, who "trains and perfects himself only in appearances,"[25] wears different faces, traverses different centuries, lives countless lives all before the curtain closes on his own. But beneath it all, he remains aware. He knows that he is only play-acting and that hidden behind the mask lives the son of a lie. He is the lie—a handful of dust clothed in the skin of a man. And in the end, all of his buffoonery, all of his passion, his love, his rebellion, his wild thirst for life—all will end in ruin. All will come to naught.

That the patriarch of the Karamazov family should be an absurd man is fitting. For, the world into which he throws his offspring is meaningless. And he confronts that meaninglessness head on. He confronts it by playing the fool. Yet his buffoonery, far from giving life "its value,"[26] as Camus would have us believe, actually causes a great deal of anguish. He suffers because of it. (He is murdered because of it.) And his sons suffer, too. Yes, Fyodor Karamazov is an absurd man. His meaning is meaninglessness. And through his actions, he imposes upon his children an oppression like no other. He neglects them, rejects them, steals from them, stifles their freedom. He is malicious and manipulative, willing to sacrifice everyone—and his sons most of all—in order to "accumulate" an ever-greater "quantity and variety of experiences."[27] His thirst for life is endless. His heart is full of "the passionate flames of revolt."[28] And his children, the brothers Karamazov, are the ones who get burned.

23. Dostoevsky, *Brothers Karamazov*, 11.
24. Camus, *Myth of Sisyphus*, 79.
25. Camus, *Myth of Sisyphus*, 80.
26. Camus, *Myth of Sisyphus*, 55.
27. Camus, *Myth of Sisyphus*, 60–61.
28. Camus, *Myth of Sisyphus*, 64.

3.

"Who doesn't wish for his father's death?" asks Ivan Karamazov.[29] And with a father like his, it is no wonder why. But the murder of Fyodor Pavlovich, as we have said, is more than a mere patricide. It is a deicide—the killing of an absurd god, a cruel author who had the audacity to write four souls out of nonexistence into a meaningless world. Yet can such a father even be called a father? Can so absurd an origin really be the character's author, his god? "It is a horrible thing to shed a father's blood," concedes Dmitri's attorney; and yet, he asks, "what is a father, a real father, what does this great word mean, what terribly great idea is contained in this appellation?"[30] Can the "absurd upbringing" suffered by the Karamazov brothers at the hands of so loathsome a man be mentioned in the same breath as this "great idea"?[31] Does the worm known as Fyodor Karamazov—"as cruel as a wicked insect"[32]—"deserve to be called a father"?[33] Oughtn't we to say that the father who begets without loving is unworthy of the name? Certainly Dmitri's attorney thinks so.

> What is a father, I was asking just now, and exclaimed that it is a great word, a precious appellation. But, gentlemen of the jury, one must treat words honestly, and I shall allow myself to name a thing by the proper word, the proper appellation: such a father as the murdered old Karamazov cannot and does not deserve to be called a father. Love for a father that is not justified by the father is an absurdity, an impossibility . . . "Fathers, provoke not your children," writes the apostle, from a heart aflame with love. I quote these holy words now not for the sake of my client, but as a reminder to all fathers . . . "Fathers, provoke not your children!" . . . Otherwise we are not fathers but enemies of our children, and they are not our

29. Dostoevsky, *Brothers Karamazov*, 686.
30. Dostoevsky, *Brothers Karamazov*, 742.
31. Dostoevsky, *Brothers Karamazov*, 742.
32. Dostoevsky, *Brothers Karamazov*, 93.
33. Dostoevsky, *Brothers Karamazov*, 744.

> children but our enemies, and we ourselves have made them our enemies![34]

Such a father—an author as absurd and oppressive as Fyodor—is rightly seen by the character as a devil to be destroyed. (Incidentally, the Devil who abuses Ivan during his descent into madness bears an unmistakable resemblance to Fyodor; he is even described—and we ought to pay special attention to this—as having "become gradually estranged from [his] children altogether.")[35] But if Fyodor is no father, only a devil, he is at least worthy of the devil's moniker. "I am a lie and the father of a lie."[36] Or, better, *the father of lies*—four lies, each of whom bears the mark (and curse) of his maker.

Ivan Fyodorovich Karamazov

"The sight of an unworthy father," asserts Dmitri's defense, "presents a young man with tormenting questions."[37] Chief among them is, "did he love me when he was begetting me . . . Did he beget me for my own sake?" And if not, "Why should I love him just because he begot me and then never loved me all my life?"[38] As has been made clear, Fyodor Karamazov did not beget his sons for their sakes. He did not love them into existence. Indeed, it would be truer to say that he brought them with malice into a malicious world. Yet in spite of this—or perhaps because of it—the Karamazov brothers cannot escape the meaninglessness inherited from their absurd origin. Each is defined by it; each sets himself in opposition to it; and each, in his own way, succumbs.

Of the four heirs to the crooked Karamazov crown, the one who "most resembles Fyodor Pavlovich in character" is Ivan.[39]

34. Dostoevsky, *Brothers Karamazov*, 744.
35. Dostoevsky, *Brothers Karamazov*, 636.
36. Dostoevsky, *Brothers Karamazov*, 44.
37. Dostoevsky, *Brothers Karamazov*, 745.
38. Dostoevsky, *Brothers Karamazov*, 745.
39. Dostoevsky, *Brothers Karamazov*, 697.

Indeed, it is Ivan "of all his children who came out resembling him most, having the same soul as him."[40] Ivan is not unaware of this fact. He recognizes the affinity he shares with his father and their fundamental agreement about the absurd nature of existence. "Fyodor Pavlovich, our papa, was a little pig," he says, "but his thinking was right."[41] (It is for this reason that Fyodor fears Ivan more than any other; he knows what atrocities an absurd man is capable of committing.[42]) The close resemblance Ivan shares with Fyodor is that which he hates most about the old man. In hating his father, he hates himself. Yet he cannot get away from himself, cannot rid himself of the father who is always with him, always in him.

From a young age, Ivan has been aware that his father is reprehensible. He has known "that it was a shame to speak of him."[43] Thus he has spent his life attempting to distance himself from him, to negate him by ignoring him, to destroy him by cutting off all forms of communication.[44] Yet soon he realizes that he cannot free himself from the stain of his birth by simply ignoring it. Something must be done. He returns to his father's house and his arrival is met with "a certain uneasiness"—from an outside perspective, it is "inexplicable"—and our narrator remarks, "Why Ivan Fyodorovich came to us then is a question I even recall asking myself at the time."[45] But those who understand the oppression Ivan has suffered at the hands of his father, the meaninglessness forced upon him by the absurdity of his birth, grasp that "this so fateful arrival, which was the start of so many consequences," was not made arbitrarily or without reason. It was, in the strictest sense of the word, a necessity. Ivan has come to destroy his god, to watch his author crumble. The desire to witness the death of Fyodor is his secret wish. And though he claims to "reserve complete freedom"

40. Dostoevsky, *Brothers Karamazov*, 632.

41. Dostoevsky, *Brothers Karamazov*, 593.

42. See Dostoevsky, *Brothers Karamazov*, 141.

43. Dostoevsky, *Brothers Karamazov*, 15.

44. See Dostoevsky, *Brothers Karamazov*, 16.

45. Dostoevsky, *Brothers Karamazov*, 117.

for himself with regards to harboring such wishes,[46] the truth is that he is not free not to wish. His wish defines him. It is the essence of who he is.

"Ivan is a grave," declares Dmitri.[47] Search the Western canon and find a metaphor as apt as that. Ivan is a grave. He houses within himself the death of his father, the death of God. This son—perhaps every son—is the grave in which his father will be entombed, the empty hollow in which his maker will be buried. Fyodor is more afraid of Ivan than of any other because he recognizes this fact. He knows that Ivan is the incarnation of his ruin.

What does it mean for Ivan to be the death of his father? What does it mean to live the death of God as one's destiny? It means, first, that there is a profound affinity between father and son, that the son is so like the father that he constitutes his undoing. And indeed this is clearly the case with Ivan. Like Fyodor, Ivan recognizes "that absurdities are all too necessary on earth"; "the world stands on absurdities."[48] And like Fyodor, he will not flee from that fact, will not escape it by means of a leap, will not rest his beliefs on the unbelievable, the unknowable, the unreal.[49] Ivan too is an absurd man. He readily admits, "I don't understand anything," and yet insists, "I no longer want to understand anything. I want to stick to the fact . . . If I wanted to understand something, I would immediately have to betray the fact, but I've made up my mind to stick to the fact."[50]

What the absurd man demands of himself, writes Camus, "is to live *solely* with what he knows, to accommodate himself to what is, and to bring in nothing that is not certain."[51] That Ivan lives this ideal is made clear by his renunciation of any belief in a "higher harmony," his insistence that "I'd rather remain with my

46. Dostoevsky, *Brothers Karamazov*, 143.

47. Dostoevsky, *Brothers Karamazov*, 110.

48. Dostoevsky, *Brothers Karamazov*, 243.

49. The kinship between Fyodor and Ivan is made explicit during a discussion they have with Alyosha. See Dostoevsky, *Brothers Karamazov*, 132–38.

50. Dostoevsky, *Brothers Karamazov*, 243.

51. Camus, *Myth of Sisyphus*, 53.

unrequited suffering and my unquenched indignation, *even if I am wrong*," than escape the absurdity of the world by putting his faith in that which he cannot comprehend.[52]

Yet Ivan is not content with mere rebellion, as Fyodor is. He is not so taken with the absurdity of life that he is willing to play the buffoon. His ideal is not Camus's, not that of an actor on the stage, a lucid idiot who imagines himself happy while rolling a stone. He wants not to rebel against the world—"one cannot live by rebellion"[53]—not to reject it, but to love it. He wants to love it without meaning, without *why*. Ivan's ideal is to "love life more than its meaning,"[54] "not with your mind, not with logic, but with your insides, your guts, [as] you love your first young strength."[55] It is to find in life an excess of life, to see in each moment "an exuberant, triumphant life in which all things, whether good or evil, are deified."[56]

> If I did not believe in life, if I were to lose faith in the woman I love, if I were to lose faith in the order of things, even if I were to become convinced, on the contrary, that everything is a disorderly, damned, and perhaps devilish chaos, if I were struck even by all the horrors of human disillusionment—still I would want to live, and as long as I have bent to this cup, I will not tear myself from it until I've drunk it all![57]

Ivan has asked himself many times, "is there such despair in the world as could overcome this wild and perhaps indecent thirst for life?"[58] Is there a depth of meaninglessness that could rob him of his passion, his love? He has "decided that apparently there is not."[59] "I want to live, and I do live, even if it be against logic. Though I do

52. Dostoevsky, *Brothers Karamazov*, 245
53. Dostoevsky, *Brothers Karamazov*, 245.
54. Dostoevsky, *Brothers Karamazov*, 231.
55. Dostoevsky, *Brothers Karamazov*, 230.
56. Nietzsche, *Birth of Tragedy*, §3.
57. Dostoevsky, *Brothers Karamazov*, 230.
58. Dostoevsky, *Brothers Karamazov*, 230.
59. Dostoevsky, *Brothers Karamazov*, 230.

not believe in the order of things, still the sticky little leaves that come out in the spring are dear to me, the blue sky is dear to me, some people are dear to me, whom one loves sometimes, would you believe it, without even knowing why . . . Sticky spring leaves, the blue sky—I love them, that's all!"[60]

No, this is not Camus's ideal, not the ideal of the absurd man. This is nearer to Nietzsche, the man who, in announcing the death of God, claims to offer the most life-affirming philosophy heretofore imagined. And yet, Camus and Nietzsche are not so far from one another. Meursault, remember, "felt ready to live it all again,"[61] to say *yes* to what was and is eternally, to live out Nietzsche's eternal recurrence. If Ivan is not the absurd man, not Fyodor, that is because he is the death of the absurd man, the overcoming of the absurd man toward a new ideal, a higher goal—the overman. He is the "man-god" born of the death of God, "exalted with the spirit of the divine," overflowing with "titanic pride," standing in the place of the God he has toppled.[62] "Since God and immortality do not exist . . . the new man is allowed to become a man-god . . . and of course, in this new rank, to jump lightheartedly over any former moral obstacle of the former slave-man, if need be. There is no law for God! Where God stands—there is the place of God! Where I stand, there at once will be the foremost place."[63]

Yes, for such an overman, everything is indeed permitted. (That Kaufmann, in a passing footnote, attempts to distance Nietzsche from Ivan on this point is, I think, telling.[64] Perhaps he is embarrassed by the Devil's retort to the Nietzschean ideal? "It's all very nice; only if one wants to swindle, why, I wonder, should one also need the sanction of truth?"[65]) Ivan and Nietzsche, it is clear, share a philosophy. Theirs is a philosophy of the future. They long

60. Dostoevsky, *Brothers Karamazov*, 230.

61. Camus, *Stranger*, 122.

62. Dostoevsky, *Brothers Karamazov*, 649.

63. Dostoevsky, *Brothers Karamazov*, 649.

64. See Nietzsche, *On the Genealogy of Morals*, §24, 150, n. 8.

65. Dostoevsky, *Brothers Karamazov*, 649.

to "destroy the idea of God,"[66] to rid the character of the oppression of his author. Their goal is to find "happiness and joy in this world only,"[67] to make "the overman . . . the meaning of the earth."[68] As Camus rightly notes, "for Nietzsche, to kill God is to become god oneself; it is to realize on this earth the eternal life of which the Gospel speaks."[69]

But can this earthly beatitude be achieved? Can the character affirm life, become god, bestow upon existence a meaning all his own? Even when absurdity abounds? For Ivan, the murder of Fyodor represents his one hope of escaping the oppression of his origin. Yet, at the very moment he leaves for Moscow and thus sanctions Fyodor's death, at the instant he throws off the shackles of the past—"I'm through with the old world forever, and may I never hear another word or echo from it; to the new world, to new places, and no looking back!"—he feels not freedom, not joy, but disgust. "Instead of delight, such darkness suddenly descended on his soul, and such grief gnawed at his heart, as he had never known before in the whole of his life."[70] His God is dead. Everything is permitted. But for that reason, the worthlessness of everything is all the more apparent.

Ivan and Nietzsche share more than a philosophy. They share a fate. In the absence of God, each individual character is left only with himself—a self he cannot bear. His meaning, he finds, is meaningless. He is the son of a lie. He is himself a lie. And "Without a firm idea of what he lives for, [he] will not consent to live . . . [he] will sooner destroy himself than remain on earth."[71] Ivan does destroy himself. His descent into madness, unfreedom, isolation, and despair represents the breaking up of a mind that has recognized the meaninglessness and inescapability of sin. Like Raskolnikov, he has "lost his bearings." He is "tormented by

66. Dostoevsky, *Brothers Karamazov*, 648.

67. Dostoevsky, *Brothers Karamazov*, 649.

68. Nietzsche, *Thus Spoke Zarathustra*, "Prologue," §3.

69. Camus, *Myth of Sisyphus*, 108.

70. Dostoevsky, *Brothers Karamazov*, 280.

71. Dostoevsky, *Brothers Karamazov*, 254.

various strange and almost entirely unexpected desires"[72] and finds himself being dragged along by "irresistible" forces.[73] He no longer has any freedom of mind or will and soon succumbs to insanity—one last pathetic attempt to flee the senselessness of his situation. Yet even when he loses his mind, still the problem persists. (The Devil who haunts Ivan, we said, is an image of Fyodor, the father he cannot escape. But if he cannot escape his maker, that is only because he cannot escape himself. The Devil is, after all, no one but Ivan—"By abusing you, I'm abusing myself! . . . You are me, myself, only with a different mug. You precisely say what I already think . . . and you're not capable of telling me anything new!"[74]) For Ivan, neither rebellion nor insanity offers any relief. He destroys himself, destroys the image of the father within, and in so doing only falls further into the grips of a meaninglessness he cannot escape.

4.

The realization that, like Nietzsche, "the most famous of God's assassins,"[75] Ivan too ends in madness elicits from Camus—a shrug. "Faced with such tragic ends, the essential impulse of the absurd mind is to ask: 'What does that prove?'"[76] The answer, of course, is nothing. For, there is nothing to be proved. But if that is in fact the case, why, we might ask, is Camus so insistent that "the risk is worth running"?[77] If being an absurd man—or striving for a higher ideal, the man-god, the overman—is indeed worth the risk of insanity, what then is the reward? "There is," we are told, "a metaphysical honor in enduring the world's absurdity."[78] For, when man endures, he realizes the great heights toward which he is

72. Dostoevsky, *Brothers Karamazov*, 275.
73. Dostoevsky, *Brothers Karamazov*, 603.
74. Dostoevsky, *Brothers Karamazov*, 638.
75. Camus, *Myth of Sisyphus*, 109.
76. Camus, *Myth of Sisyphus*, 109.
77. Camus, *Myth of Sisyphus*, 109.
78. Camus, *Myth of Sisyphus*, 93.

capable of ascending. "Every man has felt himself to be the equal of a god at certain moments."[79] In such moments, "How can one fail to realize that in this vulnerable universe everything that is human and solely human assumes a more vivid meaning?"[80]

A more vivid meaning! There you have it. And now we see what the stakes have been all along. Now we know where bold lucidity gets you. We would be justified, I think, in wondering whether we have been made the victims of an elaborate joke. Has Camus the court jester been pulling our noses? We have been told in all too convincing terms that life is meaningless. It is, we have been assured, utterly absurd. And now, *Voila!* Meaning. Finite meaning, to be sure. Human meaning. But meaning all the same. Meaning that makes life worth living, that gives life its value.[81] Meaning that transforms into "a rule of life" that which had been "an invitation to death."[82] Meaning that staves off suicide. Oh, if only the character had recourse to such saving comforts! If only meaning could be conjured up, pulled from a hat or found hidden behind your ear by those who have mastered the philosopher's secret art—sleight of hand.

In *The Birth of Tragedy*, Nietzsche recounts the story of King Midas who went hunting in the forest for Silenus, companion to Dionysus.

> When Silenus at last fell into his hands, the king asked what was the best and most desirable of all things for man. Fixed and unmovable, the demigod said not a word, till at last, urged by the king, he gave a shrill laugh and broke out into these words: "Oh, wretched ephemeral race, children of chance and misery, why do you compel me to tell you what it would be most expedient for you not to hear? What is best of all is utterly beyond

79. Camus, *Myth of Sisyphus*, 88.
80. Camus, *Myth of Sisyphus*, 88.
81. See Camus, *Myth of Sisyphus*, 55.
82. Camus, *Myth of Sisyphus*, 64.

> your reach: not to be born, not to *be*, to be *nothing*. But the second best for you is—to die soon."[83]

That Nietzsche and Ivan aim to reverse this horrible truth, that theirs is a philosophy of life-affirmation, of living life to the fullest, has been discussed at length above. Yet each ends in madness. Their ideal is never realized. The wisdom of Silenus proves too much for any one character to bear. In the face of so cruel and crushing a fate, when one is confronted by the sheer meaninglessness of existence, is the flight into insanity really so different from others means of escape? Is it so different from suicide?

The absurd hero is, Camus insists, the opposite of the man who dies by choice. "It may be thought that suicide follows revolt—but wrongly"; to take one's own life is to "elude the problem."[84] "Suicide . . . is acceptance at the extreme."[85] "The absurd man," on the other hand, "can only drain everything to the bitter end, and deplete himself."[86] Yes. At least until he loses his mind. (In considering the implications of this ideal, Ivan, to his credit, is more honest. He recognizes the likelihood that his passion for life will fade, that "disillusionment" and "aversion to life" will win the day—"by the age of thirty, I will probably drop the cup, even if I haven't emptied it, and walk away."[87]) What the story of the Karamazov brothers reveals is that suicide is not remote from rebellion. The two are not unrelated. They are, in fact, brothers. Or, at very least, half-brothers. Both are born of the character's confrontation with his absurd origin. Both represent a meaningless revolt against the ridiculous world into which the character has been thrown.

83. Nietzsche, *Birth of Tragedy*, §3.

84. Camus, *Myth of Sisyphus*, 54.

85. Camus, *Myth of Sisyphus*, 54.

86. Camus, *Myth of Sisyphus*, 55.

87. Dostoevsky, *Brothers Karamazov*, 230.

5.

Pavel Fyodorovich Smerdyakov

Which brings us to Smerdyakov—

"Killing yourself," writes Camus, "amounts to confessing. It is confessing that life is too much for you or that you do not understand it";[88] "Dying voluntarily implies that you have recognized, even instinctively, the ridiculous character of . . . the absence of any profound reason for living, the insane character of . . . daily agitation, and the uselessness of suffering."[89] Yet if suicide is a confession, it is often an unconscious one. "Rarely is suicide committed . . . through reflection";[90] "An act like this is prepared within the silence of the heart, as is a great work of art. The man himself is ignorant of it. One evening he pulls the trigger or jumps."[91] Of the few characters who do become aware of the meaninglessness of existence, fewer still follow their logic to its ultimate end. Yet one such character—conscious, rebellious, consistent—appears in the pages of *The Brothers Karamazov*. His example is illustrative. His life means as little as his death. He is a "stinking lackey,"[92] a dog who dies "like a dog"[93]—that is, in obscurity, without master or meaning, forgotten and alone.

Smerdyakov, it should be noted, is not unaware of his fate. No, he, better than most, grasps the horrible wisdom of Silenus. He lives with it. And in the end, he dies with it. Not only does he reject his home, his lot in life, the only world he knows,[94] he rejects the absurdity of the world itself, the painful senselessness of existence. "I'd have let them kill me in the womb, so as not to come

88. Camus, *Myth of Sisyphus*, 5.

89. Camus, *Myth of Sisyphus*, 5–6.

90. Camus, *Myth of Sisyphus*, 5.

91. Camus, *Myth of Sisyphus*, 4.

92. Dostoevsky, *Brothers Karamazov*, 225.

93. Dostoevsky, *Brothers Karamazov*, 661.

94. "I hate all of Russia, Maria Kondratievna" (Dostoevsky, *Brothers Karamazov*, 225).

out into the world at all."[95] Yet for all of this, he is no worse off than any other. His life is meaningless, to be sure; but so too is everyone else's. And thus with a contempt born of pride, he can look at his fellow characters and ask, "[H]ow is he any better than me?"[96] (If another character is "better" than him, it is only "because he's a lot stupider than me"—that is, unable or unwilling to recognize the insane character of meaningless living.)

This proud contempt—this *scorn*, to use the language of Camus—signals Smerdyakov's affinity with the ideal we have just considered. (It is no accident that Ivan and Smerdyakov are co-conspirators in the murder of their father.) The would-be man-god and the suicide are siblings, both devoid of blinders, born of a conscious confrontation with the abyss. Smerdyakov, like Ivan, is the son of a lie. But unlike Ivan—who, because he knows the name of his father, believes he can escape the oppression of his origin—Smerdyakov harbors no grand illusions. Ivan wants to kill his God. Smerdyakov wants only to kill himself.[97] His despair is not hidden from him, not concealed behind some misbegotten belief that he can stand in the place of God. He wants to "consume himself," to "get rid of himself," to "reduce himself to nothing."[98] But he cannot not be, cannot be nothing, and so he must settle for what is second best. Suicide is his ideal.

For Smerdyakov, the oppression of his origin comes not from its absurdity but its obscurity. It is oppressive because it is unknown. Fyodor Pavlovich is his father—*perhaps*. But the lie runs deep. So deep, in fact, that Smerdyakov is forced to grow up "without a father,"[99] never knowing "who was the sinner," "who was the offender" that defiled his mother and forced him out into

95. Dostoevsky, *Brothers Karamazov*, 224.

96. Dostoevsky, *Brothers Karamazov*, 225.

97. Whether or not Smerdyakov acts on this desire—there is ample evidence to suggest that he is actually killed by his raving half-brother Ivan—matters little. We are considering the values by which characters govern their actions, not the actions themselves.

98. Kierkegaard, *Sickness unto Death*, 19.

99. Dostoevsky, *Brothers Karamazov*, 224.

the world.[100] True, "the rumor pointed straight at Fyodor Pavlovich, and kept pointing at him"; but that absurd old man "never owned up to it,"[101] even in spite of the fact that he took it upon himself to name the bastard child and, in so doing, to act as if he was Smerdyakov's origin. The name he bestowed upon the boy underscores the point—"he called him Smerdyakov, after the name of his mother, Lizaveta Smerdyashcaya."[102]

Smerdyakov is the son of Stinking Lizaveta, literally "son of the stinking one."[103] He has no father, no foundation, he was pulled up out of the abyss. (The servant Grigory sums it up thusly, "You are not a human being, you were begotten of bathhouse slime, that's who you are."[104]) Even his name is given *ex nihilo*, "invented" on a whim by a natural-born buffoon. Smerdyakov is a fatherless stray, "born of the devil's son,"[105] child of a lie. He may consider himself to be "the illegitimate son of Fyodor Pavlovich" and perhaps "there are facts to support it,"[106] but he does not know—will never know—where he came from, why he was begotten, the meaning of his life. He lives without meaning, without *why*. He is suspended out over the abyss—the nothingness from which he came and to which he will return—and his only certainty is that death awaits him in the end.

Is it any wonder that Smerdyakov lives as "a decidedly spiteful being, enormously ambitious, vengeful, and burning with envy"?[107] Is it any wonder that he is "terribly unsociable and taciturn," "arrogant," lacking in gratitude, he seems "to despise everyone"?[108] If it is true that Smerdyakov loves "no one but himself and his respect

100. Dostoevsky, *Brothers Karamazov*, 99.
101. Dostoevsky, *Brothers Karamazov*, 99.
102. Dostoevsky, *Brothers Karamazov*, 100.
103. See Dostoevsky, *Brothers Karamazov*, 100, n. 2.
104. Dostoevsky, *Brothers Karamazov*, 124.
105. Dostoevsky, *Brothers Karamazov*, 100.
106. Dostoevsky, *Brothers Karamazov*, 738.
107. Dostoevsky, *Brothers Karamazov*, 738.
108. Dostoevsky, *Brothers Karamazov*, 124.

for himself [is] peculiarly high,"[109] that is because he spends his life "rebelling against [his] nativity."[110] "I could have been even better, miss, and I'd know a lot more, if it wasn't for my destiny ever since childhood. I'd have killed a man in a duel with a pistol for calling me low-born, because I came from Stinking Lizaveta without a father."[111]

Smerdyakov "detest[s] his position as compared with that of his master's legitimate children" and he blames his misfortune on the accident of his birth.[112] Yet ironically, it is he who inherits at birth—and as a consequence thereof—that which his brother Ivan so desperately desires—autonomy, the independence to determine himself. (Smerdyakov, remember, has no relations; his mother died in childbirth, his father will not recognize him as his legitimate son, his siblings receive their inheritance "while he is just the cook."[113]) He is self-sufficient of necessity. He has no one. He needs no one. He is alone. Thus he must make himself, must fashion himself into the man he wants to be.[114]

Yet the truth that Ivan declares by his insanity is the horrible wisdom that Smerdyakov already knows—autonomy brings not freedom but despair, independence means nothing in a meaningless world. In fact, the truly sovereign individual—the character born without father, author, god—is not a character at all. He is an isolated "unit," uncared for and unknown. ("You are not a human being, you were begotten of bathhouse slime."[115]) The reality

109. Dostoevsky, *Brothers Karamazov*, 738.

110. Dostoevsky, *Brothers Karamazov*, 224.

111. Dostoevsky, *Brothers Karamazov*, 224.

112. "[H]e hated his origin, was ashamed of it, and gnashed his teeth when he recalled that he was 'descended from Stinking Lizaveta'" (Dostoevsky, *Brothers Karamazov*, 738).

113. Dostoevsky, *Brothers Karamazov*, 738.

114. The emptiness of his ambitions underscores the meaninglessness of all such attempts at self-affirmation. "He dreamed of going to France and remaking himself as a Frenchman . . . Enlightenment he regarded as good clothes, clean shirt fronts, and polished boots" (Dostoevsky, *Brothers Karamazov*, 738).

115. Dostoevsky, *Brothers Karamazov*, 124.

that confronts Smerdyakov and Ivan alike, the cruel fate that leads each to his tragic end, is that in the face of an absurd existence, the individual character is not free to create meaning, not capable of fashioning himself as he chooses, and his every attempt to do so only intensifies his despair.

Unlike Ivan—who, in striving for "the fullness of self-definition," "does not see, madman as he is, that . . . he sinks into suicidal impotence"—Smerdyakov is born with an autonomy that amounts to nothing more than "complete isolation."[116] He does not strive "to experience the fullness of life within himself." He does not seek "seclusion in his own hole," "pushing himself away from people and pushing people away from himself."[117] He is the hole—a bottomless pit of meaninglessness and despair. He knows already that "wishing to experience the fullness of life" within oneself leads "not to the fullness of life but full suicide."[118] He refuses the charade, will not play a ridiculous part, and instead goes straight for the goal. But if his end is "inevitable and despicable,"[119] it is no worse than Ivan's madness, the mental suicide of a character crushed by the unbearable weight of sin. Neither is it any better. In fact, the two are one and the same. Both suicide and rebellion reveal that the meaninglessness of existence is too much bear. And yet, in the end, both show that it cannot be escaped.

116. Dostoevsky, *Brothers Karamazov*, 303.

117. Dostoevsky, *Brothers Karamazov*, 303.

118. Dostoevsky, *Brothers Karamazov*, 303.

119. Camus, *Myth of Sisyphus*, 123.

Chapter 6

Faith and Freedom

1.

In his reading of *The Brothers Karamazov*, Camus takes issue with Dostoevsky's great novel. For, in spite of the fact that "no one so much as Dostoevsky has managed to give the absurd world such familiar and tormenting charms," in spite of the fact that *The Brothers Karamazov* represents "an amazing creation in which . . . creatures of fire and ice seem so familiar to us" and "The passionate world of indifference that rumbles in their hearts does not seem at all monstrous to us,"[1] still, "It is not an absurd work that is involved here, but a work that propounds the absurd problem."[2] After all, any attempt to "transform into joyful certainty the suffering of a lifetime"[3] is an attempt to negate the absurd. Like Ivan, the absurd man remains with unrequited suffering. He refuses consolations. He will not hope. Yet at the end of Dostoevsky's masterwork, we are given more than hope. We are given a "complete metaphysical reversal," a meaning that resolves the absurd by denying it, that attempts to do away with meaninglessness by insisting that it does not exist.

1. Camus, *Myth of Sisyphus*, 110.
2. Camus, *Myth of Sisyphus*, 112.
3. Camus, *Myth of Sisyphus*, 111.

> . . . in the last pages of his last novel, at the conclusion of that gigantic combat with God, some children ask Aliocha: "Karamazov, is it true what religion says, that we shall rise from the dead, that we shall see one another again?" And Aliocha answers: "Certainly, we shall see one another again, we shall joyfully tell one another everything that has happened." Thus Kirilov, Stavrogin, and Ivan are defeated. *The Brothers Karamazov* replies to *The Possessed*. And it is indeed a conclusion. Aliocha's case is not ambiguous . . . "We shall joyfully tell one another everything that has happened." Thus again Kirilov's pistol rang out somewhere in Russia, but the world continued to cherish its blind hopes. Men did not understand "that."[4]

For Camus, the faith—nay, the certainty—expressed by the youngest Karamazov brother amounts to a kind of philosophical suicide; it represents a renunciation of the absurd, a hope that is no longer anchored in experience, that evades this world by leaping into the next. "What contradicts the absurd in that work . . . is not its Christian character but rather its announcing a future life."[5]

As with the works of Kierkegaard—whom Camus has already unhorsed for fleeing the absurd with his *leap of faith*[6]—so "Here, too, the leap is touching and gives its nobility to the art that inspires it."[7] Yet, touching though it may be, the leap is also pernicious; it robs the character of his highest dignity, his ability to stare meaninglessness in the face and refuse to blink. "The leap in all its forms, rushing into the divine or the eternal, surrendering to the illusions of the everyday or of the idea—all these screens hide the absurd."[8] It is, therefore, "no matter of indifference to find hope coming back [into *The Brothers Karamazov*] under one of its most

4. Camus, *Myth of Sisyphus*, 110–111.

5. Camus, *Myth of Sisyphus*, 112.

6. "The struggle is eluded . . . This leap is an escape" (Camus, *Myth of Sisyphus*, 35).

7. Camus, *Myth of Sisyphus*, 111.

8. Camus, *Myth of Sisyphus*, 91.

touching guises. That shows the difficulty of the absurd *ascesis*."[9] It shows how "the absurd man is tempted . . . He is asked to leap."[10] And if he does leap, if he puts his faith in something higher than himself, in his author, his god, then he "exchanges his divinity for happiness,"[11] the hard-won triumph of rebellion for the comfort that certainty alone can provide. He forgoes the only path to authentic meaning—the absurd *via crucis*, if you will—and becomes, once more, a puppet on a string.

But the "joyful certainty" voiced through the mouth of Alyosha is, for Camus, more troubling still. For, it does not represent the willful blindness of a character unable to bear the sight of the absurd. It is not Kierkegaard's "spiritual leap which basically escapes consciousness"[12] by refusing to remain at "the subtle instant that precedes the leap," the "extreme danger" of "that dizzying crest."[13] It is, rather, a curse imposed upon the character from without. According to Camus, Alyosha does not leap. He is pushed, forced off the ledge by the one who made him. "Here is a work which, in a chiaroscuro more gripping than the light of day, permits us to seize man's struggle against his hopes. Having reached the end, the creator makes his choice against his characters . . . The surprising reply of the creator to his characters, of Dostoevsky to Kirilov, can indeed be summed up thus: existence is illusory *and* it is eternal."[14] The god has spoken. The final word belongs to him. The world of the novel is a fiction—*his* creation—and its meaning was, is, and ever shall be his alone.

9. Camus, *Myth of Sisyphus*, 113.

10. Camus, *Myth of Sisyphus*, 52–53.

11. Camus, *Myth of Sisyphus*, 111.

12. Camus, *Myth of Sisyphus*, 59.

13. Camus, *Myth of Sisyphus*, 50.

14. Camus, *Myth of Sisyphus*, 112.

2.

Dmitri Fyodorovich Karamazov

Before we address Camus's challenge to *The Brothers Karamazov* on the whole and to Alyosha in particular, we ought first to offer a few words on the leap of faith. In order to do so, we will, for the time being, leave behind our discussion of Alyosha (who, as we shall see, represents not faith but an ideal heretofore unknown). First, we will consider the eldest of the Karamazov brothers, Dmitri, perhaps the most faithful character in all of Dostoevsky's corpus. Unlike Alyosha—whose faith is often vexed by "tormenting contradictions,"[15] "vagueness and confusion," "strain"[16]—Dmitri is "a very simple-hearted man,"[17] a man who believes in miracles,[18] "in [the] miracle of divine Providence,"[19] who needs "someone higher to forgive [him]."[20] Dmitri is a man of faith. Indeed, we ought not to allow the coarse, even grotesque manner with which he carries himself to deceive us. Even if we take seriously his self-appraisal, "I loved depravity, I also loved the shame of depravity. I loved cruelty: am I not a bedbug, an evil insect? In short—a Karamazov!"[21]—an assessment that is more than validated by his actions—still, we must recognize that this in no way undermines his faith. (The distinction made above between sin and immorality holds for the inverse as well. Faith and morality might be enemies so alien are they to one another.) After all, "man is broad, even too broad"[22]—and the man of faith most of all.

We said above that the Karamazovs are "capable of containing all possible opposites and of contemplating both abysses at once,

15. Dostoevsky, *Brothers Karamazov*, 143.

16. Dostoevsky, *Brothers Karamazov*, 187.

17. Dostoevsky, *Brothers Karamazov*, 368.

18. "You worked miracles, O Lord, for sinners just like me!" (Dostoevsky, *Brothers Karamazov*, 437).

19. Dostoevsky, *Brothers Karamazov*, 121.

20. Dostoevsky, *Brothers Karamazov*, 105.

21. Dostoevsky, *Brothers Karamazov*, 109.

22. Dostoevsky, *Brothers Karamazov*, 108.

the abyss above us, an abyss of lofty ideals, and the abyss beneath us, an abyss of the lowest and foulest degradation."[23] But of the inheritors of this "unnatural mixture," of the heirs to Fyodor's absurd throne, none descend as low as Dmitri. And none strive for such heights. Like his father and brothers, this character is not unaware of "What terrible tragedies realism inflicts on people."[24] No, he is the author of more than one such tragedy. But unlike his relations, Dmitri fully grasps the utter helplessness of his situation. Not only does he recognize the absurdity of characterly living—that is, as Calderón says, that "the greatest sin is to have been born"—he sees just how futile resistance is. He will not rebel. He knows himself too well to idealize revolt. All he can do is repent and trust that salvation comes to those in need of saving.

For Dmitri, faith is neither a consolation nor a cure. It is a recognition that "the devil is struggling with God, and the battlefield is the human heart."[25] It is the realization that grace comes from without whereas wretchedness is always the character's own.

> There's so terribly much suffering for man on earth, so terribly much grief for him! Don't think I'm just a brute of an officer who drinks cognac and goes whoring. No, brother, I hardly think of anything . . . but that fallen man . . . because I myself am such a man . . . when I fall into the abyss, I go straight into it, head down and heels up, and I'm even pleased that I'm falling in just such a humiliating position, and for me I find it beautiful. And so in that very shame I suddenly begin a hymn. Let me be cursed, let me be base and vile, but let me also kiss the hem of that garment in which my God is clothed; let me be following the devil at the same time, but still I am also your son, Lord, and I love you, and I feel a joy without which the world cannot stand and be.[26]

23. Dostoevsky, *Brothers Karamazov*, 699.
24. Dostoevsky, *Brothers Karamazov*, 376.
25. Dostoevsky, *Brothers Karamazov*, 108.
26. Dostoevsky, *Brothers Karamazov*, 106–7.

The man of faith is a man of contradictions. He is a man of strife and contention. A man whose life is ever suspended, caught in the tension between his God and the godlessness of his own heart. "It's . . . fearful when someone who already has the ideal of Sodom in his soul does not deny the ideal of the Madonna either, and his heart burns with it, verily, verily burns, as in his young, blameless years."[27] Fearful because such a one as this, such a broad and singular individual, can neither make himself understandable to others nor understand himself. He lives in anxiety, in fear and trembling, where "the shores converge, [where] all contradictions live together"—"God gave us only riddles . . . I'm a very uneducated man, brother, but I've thought about it a lot. So terribly many mysteries! Too many riddles oppress man on earth."[28]

For Camus, "The leap does not represent an extreme danger as Kierkegaard would like it to do."[29] Yet this is because Camus misunderstands the leap. As his critique of Dostoevsky makes clear, he considers Alyosha to be an exemplar of faith, not Dmitri. But it is Dmitri who, in Kierkegaardian terms, puts his faith in the absurd. It is Dmitri who "expect[s] the impossible,"[30] who "finds pleasure in everything, takes part in everything . . . enjoys everything."[31] And not just when in "delirium" like during the infamous "feast of feasts" in Mokroye, at which Dmitri is described as being "in his natural element . . . and the more absurd it all became, the more his spirits rose."[32] No, even when he has been detained, interrogated,

27. Dostoevsky, *Brothers Karamazov*, 108.

28. Dostoevsky, *Brothers Karamazov*, 108.

29. Camus, *Myth of Sisyphus*, 50.

30. Kierkegaard, *Fear and Trembling*, 16. Cf. "Strangely enough, it would seem that after such a decision nothing was left for him but despair; for how could one suddenly come up with so much money, especially such a pauper as he? Nevertheless, to the very end he kept hoping that he would get the three thousand, that the money would come to him, that it would somehow fly down to him by itself, from the sky no less . . . Yes, perhaps with such people, precisely in such situations, it is the most impossible and fantastic enterprises that seem to offer the best possibilities" (Dostoevsky, *Brothers Karamazov*, 376).

31. Kierkegaard, *Fear and Trembling*, 39.

32. Dostoevsky, *Brothers Karamazov*, 432.

and charged with murder, still his heart is ablaze "with a sort of rapturous gratitude" for the supreme "kindness" showed him by one of his jailers who put a pillow under his head while he was sleeping.[33]

Yet this "tenderness" which wells up in Dmitri and opens him to "a joy without which the world cannot stand and be" is not some naïve sentimentality. Nor is it an escapism that denies "the irony of fate."[34] No, Dmitri is the first to recognize that life is "a tragedy"; he readily admits "how dishonorable it all is!"[35] Like Kierkegaard's knight of faith, he too "drains the deep sadness of life in infinite resignation . . . he has felt the pain of renouncing everything, the most precious thing in the world."[36] (Having lost Grushenka—"the queen of [his] soul," the one he "cannot not love"[37]—Dmitri resolves "to make way" so that she can marry another.[38]) He lives with "the distress, the anxiety, the paradox" of the absurd.[39] "And yet," Kierkegaard tells us, "faith is this paradox."[40] It is the very contradiction that Dmitri embodies, the contradiction that enables the individual character to be both hopelessly, helplessly trapped in sin and, at the same time, to sing out with "foolishness," "madness," and "love"[41]—"Glory to the Highest in the world, / Glory to the Highest in me."[42]

3.

Dmitri is a knight of faith. He makes, and continues to make, the leap. But contrary to Camus's reading, this leap is not akin to

33. Dostoevsky, *Brothers Karamazov*, 508.
34. Dostoevsky, *Brothers Karamazov*, 377.
35. Dostoevsky, *Brothers Karamazov*, 376–77.
36. Kierkegaard, *Fear and Trembling*, 40.
37. Dostoevsky, *Brothers Karamazov*, 412.
38. Dostoevsky, *Brothers Karamazov*, 402.
39. Kierkegaard, *Fear and Trembling*, 65.
40. Kierkegaard, *Fear and Trembling*, 56.
41. Kierkegaard, *Fear and Trembling*, 16–17.
42. Dostoevsky, *Brothers Karamazov*, 103.

a flight from the absurdity of existence. No, to leap is to plunge straight into the absurd, head down and heels up. It is to "leap into life,"[43] to know "the blessedness of infinity" and yet to remain "in finitude," to "delight in it as if finitude were the surest thing of all."[44] "Temporality, finitude—that is what it is all about!"[45] Indeed, could a truer statement be made of Dmitri than to say that he "belongs entirely to finitude . . . He belongs entirely to the world"?[46] And yet, in the secret depths of his soul, when no one is watching, this "frivolous, wild, passionate"[47] man whispers to himself, "Lord, take me in all my lawlessness, but do not judge me. Let me pass without your judgment . . . Do not judge me, for I have condemned myself; do not judge me, for I love you, Lord! I am loathsome but I love you: if you send me to hell, even there I will love you, and from there I will cry that I love you unto ages of ages."[48] Yes, Dmitri has faith. He makes the leap. He lives the tension, the anxiety, the paradox—at least for a time.

If you want to know whether a philosophy is livable, look at the life of the one who espouses it—that's a maxim. And it is just what we have been doing from the start. Take Ivan's philosophy, for instance; we've said that it is all well and good except that it drove poor Ivan mad. There's a clue. In life, as in literature, the greatness of a work is judged by its ending. Or consider, once more, the ideal offered by that godly gadfly in Athens; it is reasonable, I think, to question the wisdom of a worldview that makes one eager to drink poison. Let us, then, in our assessment of the leap, consider Dmitri's life—and, in particular, where his life ends up.

At the close of *The Brothers Karamazov*, Dmitri is in prison. He sits in a cell, a condemned man. And to what end? He is innocent of the crime—that much is certain. (Whether it was Smerdyakov or Ivan or Rakitin or another character who smashed in old

43. Kierkegaard, *Fear and Trembling*, 41.

44. Kierkegaard, *Fear and Trembling*, 40.

45. Kierkegaard, *Fear and Trembling*, 49.

46. Kierkegaard, *Fear and Trembling*, 39.

47. Dostoevsky, *Brothers Karamazov*, 12.

48. Dostoevsky, *Brothers Karamazov*, 412.

Fyodor's head—the symbolic nature of which is emphasized all the more when we remember that "Living is keeping the absurd alive. Keeping it alive is, above all, contemplating it"[49]—is, to my mind, open for conjecture.) What meaning can there be in his getting "a twenty-year taste of the mines"?[50] What meaning in abject bondage? Dmitri is at the mercy of a senseless and crushing fate—there is no more to it than that. He is being sent by his author to the hell of which he promised "even there I will love you, and from there I will cry that I love you unto ages of ages." Yet when confronted with the prospects of hell, a real, torturous hell—not the hell his father speaks of so flippantly[51]—Dmitri buckles. Finitude is too much for him. He can no longer make the absurd leap. He loses his faith. He must escape.

Shortly after being arrested, Dmitri insists that he is willing to "let God decide" his fate.[52] He is ready to "accept the torment of accusation and of . . . disgrace before all" because he realizes that "we are all cruel, we are all monsters, we all make people weep, mothers and nursing babies, but of all . . . I am the lowest vermin!" He wants "to suffer and be purified by suffering!" "Every day of my life I've been beating my breast and promising reform, and every day I've done the same vile things. I understand now that for men such as I a blow is needed, a blow of fate, to catch them as with a noose and bind them by an external force. Never, never would I have risen by myself! But the thunder has struck . . . I accept my punishment."[53]

Yet when the verdict comes in and his God has settled on a senseless fate, Dmitri changes his tune. He is ready to "flee,"

49. Camus, *Myth of Sisyphus*, 54.

50. Dostoevsky, *Brothers Karamazov*, 753.

51. "Surely it's impossible, I think, that the devils will forget to drag me down to their place with their hooks when I die. And then I think: hooks? Where do they get them? What are they made of? Iron? Where do they forge them? Have they got some kind of factory down there?" (Dostoevsky, *Brothers Karamazov*, 25).

52. Dostoevsky, *Brothers Karamazov*, 509.

53. Dostoevsky, *Brothers Karamazov*, 509.

"escape"; "how could Mitka Karamazov not run away?"[54] In the penultimate chapter, titled *For a Moment the Lie Became Truth*, Dmitri exclaims from behind bars that he loves Alyosha "for always telling the whole and complete truth and never hiding anything."[55] He says this after Alyosha has convinced him that the uselessness of his suffering is too much to bear; he ought indeed to escape. "You know very well I won't lie to you," Alyosha says. "Listen, then: you're not ready, and such a cross is not for you. Moreover, unready as you are, you don't need such a martyr's cross . . . such a cross is too much for you . . . Heavy burdens are not for everyone, for some they are impossible."[56] And yet faith, we have been told, expects the impossible. Faith makes the impossible possible.[57] It bears all things, believes all things, hopes all things, endures all things—by virtue of the absurd.[58]

Nevertheless, Alyosha, we must concede, is correct. Dmitri is incapable of assuming the full weight of meaninglessness. He was not made to bear the senselessness of sin. That hell is just too much. (How it is that Alyosha can lie to Dmitri about the demands of faith, yet in such a way that his lie *becomes truth*, will be taken up in subsequent sections.) No character can take upon himself the monstrous burden of existence. None can carry the cross of life. Each, as has been shown, will inevitably falter and succumb. The leap—like absurdity, rebellion, and suicide—ends in escape. (It is no coincidence that Dmitri, too, has considered suicide and has come frightfully close to committing it.) The leap is initiated by the advent of an "external force"[59]—as Kierkegaard puts it, "By my own strength I cannot get the least little thing that belongs

54. Dostoevsky, *Brothers Karamazov*, 764.

55. Dostoevsky, *Brothers Karamazov*, 764.

56. Dostoevsky, *Brothers Karamazov*, 763–64.

57. Kierkegaard, *Fear and Trembling*, 44.

58. "[T]he movement of faith must continually be made by virtue of the absurd, but yet in such a way, please note, that one does not lose [nor flee from] the finite but gains it whole and intact" (Kierkegaard, *Fear and Trembling*, 37).

59. Dostoevsky, *Brothers Karamazov*, 509.

to finitude."[60] At the end comes its consequence—either flight or submission.

In the final pages of *The Brothers Karamazov*, we observe a complete reversal in Dmitri's ideal. No longer is he ready, "from the depths of the earth . . . [to] start singing a tragic hymn to God, in whom there is joy!"[61] No longer can he boldly proclaim, "what is suffering? I'm not afraid of it, even if it's numberless."[62] No, now he is "not ready! Not strong enough to take it! I wanted to sing a 'hymn,' yet I can't stand [confinement]!"[63] He is imprisoned. Trapped in the hell of despair with no hope and a faltering faith. Escape has become his ideal. Flight at any cost—even if it means submitting to the indignity of exchanging his faith for happiness; even if it means allowing another to "rule over him" as, indeed, Alyosha prophesied he would.[64]

4.

Just as Alyosha prophesied he would. And this is not the only of the young novice's predictions to come true. Far from it. Time and time again, the "hero" of this novel speaks with certainty about the future—with, one might say, a preternatural conviction—only to be proved right in the pages that follow. It is an odd habit that he evidently inherited from his spiritual father, Zosima, who himself is known for making bold declarations about things to come. Yet, what can justify a character speaking so confidently—as if he has

60. Kierkegaard, *Fear and Trembling*, 49.

61. Dostoevsky, *Brothers Karamazov*, 592.

62. Dostoevsky, *Brothers Karamazov*, 592.

63. Dostoevsky, *Brothers Karamazov*, 763.

64. "Alyosha sensed by some sort of instinct that a character like Katerina Ivanovna must rule, and that she could only rule over a man like Dmitri . . . For only Dmitri (in the long run, let us say) might finally submit to her 'for his own happiness'" (Dostoevsky, *Brothers Karamazov*, 187). And he does submit to her. She is the one who orchestrates his escape. See Dostoevsky, *Brothers Karamazov*, 757–61.

received "a sort of illumination"[65]—of events waiting to unfold, events that exist nowhere, perhaps, but in the dark recesses of the author's heart? To answer this question, we will first have to pose another: Who is the author of *The Brothers Karamazov*? Who is it that narrates this tale?

Alexei Fyodorovich Karamazov

We said above that for the individual character, the author and the father are one. Each external authority is interchangeable with every other. Each attempts to force meaning upon the character from without. Yet this novel is clearly not the work of Fyodor Karamazov. That absurd old buffoon contented himself with playing a ridiculous part. He was an actor, not an author; unwilling to house his children, let alone create a world for them to inhabit. And "Needless to say"—a phrase used by those ready to say something all the same—the author "is not Dostoevsky."[66] But if neither of them, then who?

Before we have set foot in the world of the novel, we are given two clues. First, the epigraph, a quotation from the Gospel of John: "Verily, verily, I say unto you, Except a corn of wheat fall into the ground and die, it abideth alone: but if it die, it bringeth forth much fruit" (an image that reveals so perfectly the idea it attempts to convey that those of a religious persuasion could be forgiven for thinking that the process of plant reproduction was created solely to provide a fitting metaphor). We will return to this epigraph momentarily. Second, the note *From the Author* that begins:

> Starting out on the biography of my hero Alexei Fyodorovich Karamazov, I find myself in some perplexity. Namely, that while I do call Alexei Fyodorovich my hero, still, I myself know that he is by no means a great man, so that I can foresee the inevitable questions, such as: What is notable about your Alexei Fyodorovich that you should choose him for your hero? What has he really done? To

65. Dostoevsky, *Brothers Karamazov*, 190.

66. Pevear, "Introduction," in Dostoevsky, *Brothers Karamazov*, xv.

> whom is he known, and for what? Why should I, the reader spend my time studying the facts of his life?[67]

In other words, was it not presumptuous on the part of the author to tell this story? What justifies its existence? What is its purpose, its meaning? And Alyosha—what of him? What means his life? What value does he have?

That the author describes Alyosha as being "a figure of an indefinite, indeterminate sort"[68] is our first hint. For, unlike the characters we have considered thus far—characters determined by the fixity of sin—Alyosha has yet to be defined. There is an unfinished quality to him, a secret potentiality lying dormant within. Whereas the others strive to "find at least some general sense in the general senselessness"—hence the ideals explicated above—Alyosha is content with being "a particular and isolated case."[69] He is not concerned with offering a philosophy that makes sense of life by ridding life of its senselessness. He is not concerned with offering a philosophy at all. He wants only to live life, his life and no one else's. He has little use for abstractions, for ideas. Ivan is ready to suffer for the sake of his ideas. Alyosha suffers by his love.[70] He seeks not explanations. He is too busy giving himself to the characters around him to be concerned with finding answers.

Strange that such a singular and seemingly thoughtless figure could be this novel's great hero. Strange that he could, according to the author, bear "within himself the heart of the whole."[71] Yet when we return to the epigraph quoted above, we begin to understand why. For, the "corn of wheat" is Alyosha—there can be no doubt about it. He is the one whose death brings forth much

67. Dostoevsky, *Brothers Karamazov*, 3.

68. Dostoevsky, *Brothers Karamazov*, 3.

69. Dostoevsky, *Brothers Karamazov*, 3.

70. Indeed, his is the sort of "active love" described by Zosima: "love your neighbors actively and tirelessly. The more you succeed in loving, the more you'll be convinced of the existence of God and the immortality of your soul" (Dostoevsky, *Brothers Karamazov*, 56). Alyosha, we are told, "could not love passively; once he loved, he immediately also began to help" (187).

71. Dostoevsky, *Brothers Karamazov*, 3.

fruit. (It is the death of his ego, his refusal to "condemn anyone for anything,"[72] for instance, that endears him to Fyodor,[73] earns him the trust of Dmitri,[74] and causes the implacable Ivan to confess, "I want to be healed by you."[75]) Yet if Alyosha is the corn, he is also the fruit born from the death of another. If he spends his days offering himself ceaselessly, it is because he bears within him the image and likeness of the one who died so that he might live.

We are told early in the text (and the point is reiterated again and again throughout) of Alyosha's "ardent love" for Father Zosima.[76] Zosima is an elder in the monastery at which Alyosha is a novice. He is Alyosha's elder, his spiritual father, which means that there exists "an indissoluble bond" between the two of them, the bond of "the one who binds and the one who is bound."[77] "An elder is one who takes your soul, your will into his soul and into his will. Having chosen an elder, you renounce your will and give it to him under total obedience and with total self-renunciation."[78] This practice is meant to be an "instrument for the moral regeneration of man from slavery to freedom."[79] Yet, as the author himself notes, the temptation for the novice to cling to his elder as a transmitter of meaning—external to be sure, moral, ethical, systematic—remains ever-present, "It is also true, perhaps, that this tested and already thousand-year-old instrument . . . may turn into a double-edged weapon, which may lead a person not to humility and ultimate self-control but, on the contrary, to the most satanic pride—that is, to fetters and not to freedom."[80]

72. Dostoevsky, *Brothers Karamazov*, 19.

73. "I really feel you're the only one in the world who hasn't condemned me, you are, my dear boy, I feel it, how can I not feel it . . . !" (Dostoevsky, *Brothers Karamazov*, 25).

74. Dostoevsky, *Brothers Karamazov*, 764.

75. Dostoevsky, *Brothers Karamazov*, 236.

76. Dostoevsky, *Brothers Karamazov*, 18.

77. Dostoevsky, *Brothers Karamazov*, 28.

78. Dostoevsky, *Brothers Karamazov*, 27.

79. Dostoevsky, *Brothers Karamazov*, 29.

80. Dostoevsky, *Brothers Karamazov*, 29.

The threat is real. And the young Alyosha is as susceptible as anyone. Yet instead of imposing upon him a rule or code to live by, Zosima works tirelessly to break Alyosha of his dependence. He reminds him time and again that he will soon "depart" (that is, die) and, in so doing, will send Alyosha out into the world to live in his absence. "As soon as God grants me to depart, leave the monastery. Leave it for good . . . You still have much journeying before you . . . You will have to endure everything before you come back again. And there will be much work to do. But I have no doubt of you, that is why I am sending you."[81] This prophecy causes Alyosha great anxiety.[82] For, in losing Zosima, he loses more than his spiritual guide; he loses (we may have guessed it) his father, his author, his God.

5.

When we first meet Alyosha, we are introduced to a simple-hearted boy, a boy with a deep faith—nay, certainty—in the order and meaning of existence. "Honest by nature, demanding the truth, seeking it and believing in it, and in that belief demanding immediate participation in it with all the strength of his soul," he resembles a disciple of Plato.[83] (Indeed, he adopts wholesale such Platonic teachings as the immortality of the soul and the maxim that no harm can come to a good man.[84]) His innocence borders on naiveté, causing him to conceal from himself the truth of what is to come, to make assurances that he has no business making. "I believe God will arrange it," he tells Dmitri, "so that there will be no horror"[85]—a far cry from the truly prophetic insights he will offer as he matures. Yet, in spite of the fact he is "afraid" to face

81. Dostoevsky, *Brothers Karamazov*, 77.

82. "[H]ow could he be left without him, how could he not see him, not hear him?" (Dostoevsky, *Brothers Karamazov*, 77).

83. Dostoevsky, *Brothers Karamazov*, 26.

84. See Dostoevsky, *Brothers Karamazov*, 26 and 101, respectively.

85. Dostoevsky, *Brothers Karamazov*, 122.

"the tormenting contradictions" forced upon him by life,[86] in spite of "his ardent prayer" that God not "explain his confusion to him," but only give him "the joyful tenderness" that precedes "a light and peaceful sleep,"[87] Alyosha is soon ripped from his dream world—the world of comfortable illusions—by the "strain," that is, the sin of existence.[88]

Yes, if it is true that "Alyosha's heart could not bear uncertainty,"[89] it is equally true that he who would bear "within himself the heart of the whole"[90] must be willing to face "vagueness and confusion,"[91] must be willing to endure and even welcome "tormenting contradictions." Zosima understands this. He knows only too well that—as Alyosha later confesses—his death will leave the young novice abandoned, alone.[92] But if the death of Zosima torments Alyosha, if it tears from him his certainty, his faith—"And, look, maybe I don't even believe in God"[93]—still, it is necessary. For, this character will never be free so long as the man to whom his soul is "welded" continues to live.

Man, Ivan's Grand Inquisitor tells us, "has no more tormenting care than to find someone to whom he can hand over as quickly as possible that gift of freedom with which the miserable creature is born."[94] Alyosha, we have seen, is no exception. (If anything, his desire to enter the monastery and "accept an eternal confession" to an elder—"one who takes your soul, your will into his soul and

86. Dostoevsky, *Brothers Karamazov*, 143.

87. Dostoevsky, *Brothers Karamazov*, 158–59.

88. "The word 'strain' . . . made him almost jump, because precisely that night, half-awake at dawn, probably in response to a dream, he had suddenly said: 'Strain, strain!'" (Dostoevsky, *Brothers Karamazov*, 186).

89. Dostoevsky, *Brothers Karamazov*, 187.

90. Dostoevsky, *Brothers Karamazov*, 3.

91. Dostoevsky, *Brothers Karamazov*, 187.

92. "[M]y friend is going, the first of men in the world is leaving the earth! If you knew, if you knew, Lise, how bound I am, how welded my soul is to this man! And now I shall be left alone" (Dostoevsky, *Brothers Karamazov*, 221).

93. Dostoevsky, *Brothers Karamazov*, 220.

94. Dostoevsky, *Brothers Karamazov*, 254.

into his will"[95]—reveals that he numbers himself among those who "will never be strong enough to manage their own freedom."[96]) Yet, even if Alyosha finds freedom "insufferable," still his author will not take it from him, will not impose upon him a law by which to live. Like the Christ figure in Ivan's poem, Zosima "thirst[s] for love that is free, and not the servile raptures of a slave before a power that has left him permanently terrified."[97] He allows Alyosha to "decide for himself, with a free heart, what is good and what is evil,"[98] and he does so with confidence—"I have no doubt of you, that is why I am sending you."[99]

Living in the absence of Zosima will mean for Alyosha living with the silence of God. It will mean living a forlorn existence, carrying the cross of absurdity, of meaninglessness, of suffering and death. And it will mean doing so without assistance or assurance, without being able to hope that the cross will be lifted. Had he desired to do so, Zosima could, as author, have "overcome freedom . . . in order to make [his characters] happy."[100] He could have forced his meaning upon the work, demanded that his characters submit, made them bring their freedom to him and lay it at his feet. After all, he knows that "nothing has ever been more insufferable for man and for human society than freedom!"[101] Yet he desires freedom all the same. For, his meaning can never be his characters' meaning and their meaning is even more worthless than his. Thus he has a choice to make—live and continue to stifle his characters by his presence or die and, through his absence, open up the possibility that they might be set free.[102]

95. Dostoevsky, *Brothers Karamazov*, 27–28.

96. Dostoevsky, *Brothers Karamazov*, 261.

97. Dostoevsky, *Brothers Karamazov*, 256.

98. Dostoevsky, *Brothers Karamazov*, 255.

99. Dostoevsky, *Brothers Karamazov*, 77.

100. Dostoevsky, *Brothers Karamazov*, 251.

101. Dostoevsky, *Brothers Karamazov*, 252.

102. Note here that freedom is only a *possibility*. For the character to be free, he must live out of his author's death, creating a meaning for himself that bears witness to the one who died that he might be free. (Said differently,

6.

In the final days of his life, Zosima reveals himself to be the author of the novel, the author of Alyosha. (It is plain from the start that the narrator is both a character in the novel—in the very first line he speaks of Alyosha as "the third son of a landowner from *our district*"[103]—and one possessing a god-like knowledge of the whole, that is, one who stands outside of the novel, who knows that which no mere character can know.) This book is the outpouring of his storyteller's heart—"He spoke of many things, he seemed to want to say everything, . . . to say all that had not been said in his life, and not only for the sake of instruction, but as if he wished to share his joy and ecstasy with all, to pour out his heart once more in this life."[104] Yet the story is not his alone. Above all, it is the story of his characters, of their suffering and their joy, their struggles, their triumphs, their love. As such, it is only right that Zosima should leave the last word to another, "bequeath it" to his "dear son," his son by adoption, Alyosha.[105]

It is of no little consequence that Zosima abdicates his authority, his authorship, and allows Alyosha to step forth as author precisely when the time has come to tell his, Zosima's, story. In a reversal reminiscent of that great and terrible teaching, the last shall be first and the first last, the self-proclaimed "biographer" of Alexei Fyodorovich invites his subject to recount the "Biographical Information" of his life, and even to edit it where he, the character, deems fit.

---

freedom always resembles the freedom of the one who forfeited his freedom, who died the death reserved for slaves.) But even those who attain such freedom—even Alyosha, for instance—can choose to plunge back into the abyss. The possibility of the loss of meaning, the possibility of meaninglessness, remains ever present. It is a temptation, a trap. Thus the free character must, at every moment, choose between the freedom to die for the freedom of others or the unfreedom of meaninglessness, the shackles of sin.

103. Dostoevsky, *Brothers Karamazov*, 7 (emphasis mine).

104. Dostoevsky, *Brothers Karamazov*, 163.

105. Dostoevsky, *Brothers Karamazov*, 170.

> Here I must note that this last talk of the elder with those who visited him on the last day of his life has been partly preserved in writing. Alexei Fyodorovich Karamazov wrote it down from memory some time after the elder's death . . . I have preferred, rather than recounting all of the details of the conversation, to limit myself to the elder's story according to the manuscript of Alexei Fyodorovich Karamazov. It will be shorter and not so tedious, though, of course, I repeat, Alyosha also took much from previous conversations and put it all together.[106]

Alyosha uses an experience from his life—which, "according to later reports," was quite different from his retelling—and turns it into "a narrative," that is, a novel within the novel. The author is now one of Alyosha's characters. Alyosha has become his author's author.

In reading Zosima's biography as written by Alyosha, we find that Zosima, the author of *The Brothers Karamazov*, contains within himself each member of the Karamazov family, the whole drama of their story. Like Fyodor, he has played the buffoon. Like Smerdyakov, he has sunk into cynicism and despair. Like Dmitri, he has known passion, debauchery, and faith. Like Ivan, he has rebelled and loved. Like Alyosha, he is free. He has found freedom in the death of another. Markel, his older brother, is to Zosima what Zosima is to Alyosha, what Alyosha will be to Kolya Krasotkin, what he already is to the members of his family. (As Alyosha says through the mouth of his author, "People are always saved after the death of him who saved them."[107]) It is in this way that we are to understand Alyosha's prophetic powers: he can speak with confidence about the future—he can even turn lies into truth—because, as a character who has been granted authorship by his author, he now tells the story, he is responsible for creating himself, for governing his fate, for shaping the future. Thus when he proclaims, "Certainly, we shall see one another again, we shall joyfully tell one another everything that has happened," he makes no leap of faith.

106. Dostoevsky, *Brothers Karamazov*, 286.

107. Dostoevsky, *Brothers Karamazov*, 322.

Rather, he speaks with the certainty of one who has the right to make such promises. He speaks as an author.

Camus, we began this chapter by saying, criticizes these final words of Alyosha's. "Having reached the end, the creator makes his choice against his characters."[108] But we now know that the creator is dead. There can be no doubt about it. We have smelt "the odor of corruption," have watched him die, have looked upon his festering corpse.[109] Alyosha's final words, then, are not those of his author, not imposed upon him from without. They are the character's own. For, in spite of the fact that he feels "anguish" and "great perturbation" at receiving no signs, no miracles following Zosima's death—only the meaninglessness of decay—Alyosha is, for the first time, free to live, free to choose, free to create meaning for himself.

It is out of the death of the author that the character can now do that which he was created to do, that which his captivity, his sin had prevented him from doing. Now, he can act. Not only does the corruption of Zosima's corpse testify in simple fashion to the solidarity the author shares with his characters (there is no question of the hoped-for miracle of *incorruptibility*), it thereby implicitly affirms that he has descended into the depths of meaninglessness, has become meaningless himself, has renounced any claims over the characters' meaning. And as much as Alyosha would like him to continue to act as his God, to stand "before him as an indisputable ideal"[110]—that is, an external meaning—he will not. For, "he who . . . was to have been exalted higher than anyone in the whole world, this very man, instead of receiving the glory that was due him, was suddenly thrown down and disgraced!"[111] Worse. He is dead. And Alyosha is forced to carry on in his absence, alone.

Shortly after the death of Zosima, Alyosha leaves the hermitage without permission, journeying out into the world as, indeed, Zosima prophesied he would. That this first choice, this

108. Camus, *Myth of Sisyphus*, 112.

109. Dostoevsky, *Brothers Karamazov*, 330.

110. Dostoevsky, *Brothers Karamazov*, 339.

111. Dostoevsky, *Brothers Karamazov*, 339.

first freedom, bears witness to the path laid before him by Zosima ought not to surprise us. Nor does it mean that the choice was made for him, forced upon him from the start. No, Zosima is dead. He can no longer exert his influence over the boy. He has left Alyosha "to decide for himself, with a free heart, what is good and what is evil, having only [his] image before him as a guide."[112] That image, the memory of Zosima's love, remains with Alyosha. It burns within him and becomes for him a kind of imperative—*live well, you have been purchased at a price.* The birth of this character has been ransomed by the death of his author. His freedom has been paid for in blood. Thus his every action carries with it an enormous responsibility. His author has died for him. He must now live in a way worthy of that death, must give himself as freely and as fully as the one who died in his stead. (Here is the key to understanding Zosima's paradoxical teaching that one ought to make himself "sincerely responsible for everything and everyone."[113]) And that is just what Alyosha does. For the remainder of the novel, he can be seen time and again pouring himself into his fellow characters, offering himself ceaselessly with patience and with love.

Prior to Zosima's burial, Alyosha returns to the hermitage to pray beside the coffin. Though only hours before he had fled the monastery filled with a "weeping, gnawing, tormenting pity," he now feels "sweetness in his heart."[114] He listens to Father Paissy read the story of the wedding at Cana, the first miracle, and at that moment, Zosima too performs his first miracle—he refuses to perform any miracles, he remains a stinking corpse. Alyosha falls asleep and dreams of his author. (Zosima's image is before him always.) When he awakes, we are told that he "no longer listened to what was being read."[115] The time for listening is over. It is now up to him to tell his own story. He approaches the coffin, looks at the dead man, waits, and, hearing nothing but the silence of the grave, the silence of God, he "suddenly turned abruptly and walked out

112. Dostoevsky, *Brothers Karamazov*, 255.

113. Dostoevsky, *Brothers Karamazov*, 320.

114. Dostoevsky, *Brothers Karamazov*, 359.

115. Dostoevsky, *Brothers Karamazov*, 362.

of the cell." "Filled with rapture, his soul longed for freedom, space, vastness."[116]

In a passage closely paralleled by Camus's description of Meursault's experience of the gentle indifference of the world, Alyosha is confronted by "Night, fresh and quiet, almost stirring, envelop[ing] the earth."[117] Yet unlike Meursault, who is ready to live in rebellion against the world, against his "brother,"

> Alyosha stood gazing and suddenly, as if he had been cut down, threw himself to the earth. He did not know why he was embracing it, he did not try to understand why he longed so irresistibly to kiss it, to kiss all of it, but he was kissing it, weeping, sobbing, and watering it with his tears, and he vowed ecstatically to love it, to love it unto ages of ages . . . What was he weeping for? Oh, in his rapture he wept even for the stars that shone on him from the abyss . . . It was as if threads from all those innumerable worlds of God came together in his soul, and it was trembling all over, "touching other worlds."[118]

Out of the death of his author, Alyosha arises anew. "He fell to the earth a weak youth and rose up a fighter, steadfast for the rest of his life, and he knew it and felt it suddenly, in that very moment of his ecstasy."[119] Now he is ready. Now he is free. He will tell his story. He will live his life. He will create himself. And his creation will be meaningful. For, it bursts from his author's death like roses from the thorns. Alyosha is ready to live. Alyosha is ready to love. Alyosha is ready to die. And his death, too, will bring forth fruit. In the world of the novel, characters are always saved after the death of him who made them.

116. Dostoevsky, *Brothers Karamazov*, 362.

117. Dostoevsky, *Brothers Karamazov*, 362.

118. Dostoevsky, *Brothers Karamazov*, 362.

119. Dostoevsky, *Brothers Karamazov*, 363.

Afterword

The Mask of Memnon

What then would have come of the novel mentioned at the start of this book? What followed the death of its author? It is perhaps a truism that the Greeks foresuffered us all, saw with gouged-out eyes the lives we grope through in the dark. Memnon was known to the Greeks. He was a man, not a god, destined to be written off the page. He was, it could be argued, an absurd man—a conqueror, a king, a fool. If Homer is to be believed, he was quite handsome. (Was he another of Camus's Don Juans?) Well, looks mean something. In the world of flesh and blood, appearance is no small consolation. But Memnon was meant to receive a greater blessing than this. The gods cared little for his warrior ethic. They did not love his nobility, his righteousness, his clear moral vision. They cared only for the man, the little man, destined as he was to fall.

The night before he was to head into battle in defense of Troy, Memnon sat feasting with the Trojans and with his men. It was a dark night, polar dark, the kind that makes of each man a solitary thing, that causes each to sink into the seclusion of himself, keeping lonely vigil in the blackness of his mind, the abyss of his desire, the hole that is his heart. Priam, noting the somber mood, leaned over to Memnon and beseeched him to say something—*anything!*—that might raise the warriors' spirits. "Lift your glass," he said. "Assure us of our victory." Memnon grunted. He raised his eyes from his plate and met Priam with his gaze. "If you want to judge my story," he said, "look not to what I say but what I do. The true storyteller lives his novel. His ink is his blood." Then he stood before his men and bowed down at their feet. He kissed the earth, he kissed their feet, he rose and lifted his glass. "Drink with me," he said. "Wine is no mean thing and friendship hard to come by." The men did as he commanded, they drank and laughed, and the night was merry and foolish.

In the morning, before Dawn had gifted the city with her blessing of crimson and gold, Priam called his generals to himself and said, "Do whatever Memnon tells you. Did you notice how your hearts burned as he spoke? He is not like the others." They agreed and followed Memnon into battle. The day was hot, bright, and filled with stinking death. And Memnon squeezed from it every drop it had to offer. As he fought, the gods smiled upon him. They smiled but did nothing. They rose up not in his defense. Nor did they take arms against him. They simply remained silent. "This one," said Zeus, "is more than a god. He is a man and we mustn't meddle." What did it take for the gods to restrain their wills? What did it take to give up the power that was theirs, to forsake their divinity? We need look no further than Memnon to find our answer. Memnon, pierced with a spear through the heart. Memnon, poured out upon the stones. Memnon, son of man, child of light, whose death cast a shadow over every immortal, whose blood bubbled up from the earth and became an unending river. The gods fell silent that day. They died so Memnon might live. They let that little man fight and they let him fail, and he was free to make of himself what he willed. And what was Memnon's response? What could it be but to offer himself in the same way? To give himself as a ransom for others?

There is a river that flows with blood—so says Quintus of Smyrna. It waters dry roots and stirs life where life has been snuffed out. In the *Posthomerica*, Quintus tells us that "each time that woeful day on which Memnon died comes round," the river of blood gives off "a loathsome stench," the unbearable smell of Memnon's "fatal wound."[1] The odor of corruption is strong. Memnon was no

1. Quintus, *Posthomerica*, II:560–70.

god. He was a man, one who descended to the depths of meaninglessness, who become meaningless himself. Yet by his death, he set others free. His friends, we are told, became birds—free to fly where they willed.[2] No one knew where they came from or where they were going, and that was the sign they were born of Memnon.

Nietzsche may have ushered in the death of God, but he retained a god all the same. In his 1886 preface to *The Birth of Tragedy*, he calls himself a "disciple of a still 'unknown God,'"[3] a supplicant at the altar of "an entirely reckless and amoral artist-god."[4] That God—the "primordial artist of the world," the "sole author and spectator" of our novelistic lives—does not simply look on from a distance, but at times enters the drama and becomes "at once subject and object, at once poet, actor, and spectator."[5] No place is this more evident, Nietzsche insists, than Greek tragedy, "all the celebrated figures of the Greek stage—Prometheus, Oedipus, etc.—are mere masks of this original hero, Dionysus . . . [B]ehind all these masks there is a deity . . . the one truly real Dionysus [who] appears in a variety of forms."[6] How meaningless, then, are these individual characters, mere masks for their blood-drunk god? How absurdly pointless, the tragic hero whose suffering is not his own?[7]

Memnon teaches a different lesson. Pierced through the heart, wounded by this life, he is not the mask of a man concealing the face of a god. No, Memnon is no Greek hero. He is a foreigner, an outsider, coming to the Greeks out of Egypt. If he veils his face, that is because he looks too human, too mortal, fated only to fall. Memnon is a man. He is just a man. But when he removes his

2. Quintus, *Posthomerica*, II:645.

3. Nietzsche, *Birth of Tragedy*, "Attempt at Self-Criticism," §3.

4. Nietzsche, *Birth of Tragedy*, "Attempt at Self-Criticism," §5.

5. Nietzsche, *Birth of Tragedy*, §5.

6. Nietzsche, *Birth of Tragedy*, §10.

7. "In truth, however, the hero is the suffering Dionysus of the Mysteries, the god experiencing in himself the agonies of individuation." (Nietzsche, *Birth of Tragedy*, §10).

mask, he reveals that oft-neglected truth that the face of a man is more radiant than the Sun.

JLB
Feast of Fools
January 1, 2019

Bibliography

Camus, Albert. *The Myth of Sisyphus*. Translated by Justin O'Brien. New York: Vintage, 1991.

———. *The Stranger*. Translated by Matthew Ward. New York: Vintage, 1988.

Dostoevsky, Fyodor. *The Brothers Karamazov*. Translated by Richard Pevear and Larissa Volokhonsky. New York: Farrar, Straus and Giroux, 2002.

———. *Crime and Punishment*. Translated by Richard Pevear and Larissa Volokhonsky. New York: Vintage Classics, 1993.

———. *Notes from Underground*. Translated by Jessie Coulson. New York: Penguin, 1972.

Kierkegaard, Søren. *Fear and Trembling*. Translated by Howard Hong and Edna Hong. Princeton: Princeton University Press, 1983.

———. *The Sickness unto Death*. Translated by Howard Hong and Edna Hong. Princeton: Princeton University Press, 1983.

Nietzsche, Friedrich. *Beyond Good and Evil*. Translated by Walter Kaufmann. New York: Vintage, 1989.

———. *The Birth of Tragedy from the Spirit of Music*. Translated by Walter Kaufmann. New York: Vintage, 1967.

———. *The Gay Science*. Translated by Walter Kaufmann. New York: Vintage, 1974.

———. *On the Genealogy of Morals and Ecce Homo*. Translated by Walter Kaufmann. New York: Vintage, 1989.

———. *Thus Spoke Zarathustra*. Translated by Walter Kaufmann. New York: Penguin, 1978.

———. *Twilight of Idols and the Anti-Christ*. Translated by R. J. Hollingdale. New York: Penguin, 1990.

Nygren, Anders. *Agape and Eros*. Chicago: University of Chicago Press, 1982.

Pevear, Richard. "Introduction." In *The Brothers Karamazov*, by Fyodor Dostoevsky, xi–xviii. New York: Farrar, Straus and Giroux, 2002.

Plato. *Five Dialogues: Euthyphro, Apology, Crito, Meno, Phaedo*. Translated by G. M. A. Grube. Indianapolis: Hackett, 2002.

Quintus of Smyrna. *The Trojan Epic: Posthomerica*. Translated by Alan James. Baltimore: John Hopkins University Press, 2007.

Sartre, Jean-Paul. *Existentialism*. In *Basic Writings of Existentialism*, edited by Gordon Marion, 341–67. New York: Modern Library, 2004.

von Balthasar, Hans Urs. *Life Out of Death: Meditations on the Paschal Mystery*. Translated by Martina Stockl. San Francisco: Ignatius, 2012.